WINDOW ON THE WEST

The Frontier Photography
of William Henry Jackson

To Betsy—
To read...
To share...
To enjoy!

[signature]

WINDOW ON THE WEST

The Frontier Photography
of William Henry Jackson

LAURIE LAWLOR

HOLIDAY HOUSE ✦ New York

For Megan, who also loves the West

(frontis) Harry Yount (1837–1924), also known as "Rocky Mountain Harry," stood atop Berthoud Pass in Colorado in 1874. Six years later he was hired as gamekeeper in Yellowstone National Park and became America's first park ranger.

(left) With considerable effort, Jackson climbed a canyon wall and peered through a rock formation called Temple of Isis to capture this view of Manitou Canyon near Colorado Springs, Colorado.

Text copyright © 1999 by Laurie Lawlor

All rights reserved

Printed in the United States of America

First Edition

The text typeface is Celestia Antiqua.

Map by Heather Saunders

Library of Congress Cataloging-in-Publication Data

Lawlor, Laurie.

Window on the West: William Henry Jackson's photographs in America, 1869–1893 / by Lauria Lawlor.—1st ed.

p. cm.

Summary: Presents the photographs taken by William Henry Jackson from 1869 to 1893, discussing his life and how his work captured and introduced the American West to the public.

ISBN 0-8234-1380-2

1. West (U.S.)—History—1860–1890—Pictorial works—Juvenile literature. 2. West (U.S.)—History—1860–1890—Juvenile literature. 3. Jackson, William Henry, 1843–1942—Juvenile literature. 4. Photographers—United States—Biography—Juvenile literature. [1. Jackson, William Henry, 1843–1942. 2. Photographers. 3. West (U.S.)—History.] I. Title.   F594.L39 1999

978-dc21   98-56083

CIP

AC

CONTENTS

INTRODUCTION
Such a Wonder Might Exist

If we use our imaginations when we examine William Henry Jackson's photographs of the American West, we can almost smell the sage and hear the wind blow. Jackson's eloquent black-and-white images taken between 1869 and 1893 have the power to transport us to a different place, a different time.

Viewers who first beheld Jackson's landscapes more than 100 years ago were even more moved and fascinated. His work provided many with their first glimpse of the West, an enormous, faraway place stretching from Canada to Mexico, from the 100th meridian to the Pacific—a total of nearly 1.5 million square miles. Everything about the West seemed big and exaggerated. Where else could be found such tall mountains, deep canyons, wild rivers, hostile deserts, and endless prairies?

Diverse yet fragile, the West has always been a region of little rain and great dryness. This aridity affected what kinds of plants and animals could survive there. Except for parts of California and the Pacific Northwest, rainfall west of the 100th meridian seldom exceeded twenty inches annually. There was not enough moisture to raise the kinds of crops traditionally grown by farmers in the East and the Midwest.

In spite of this drawback, the West has always beckoned irresistibly. Here was the Land of Begin Again, with wide open spaces for an unlimited number of ranches and farms and bonanzas of mineral wealth just waiting to be discovered. Jackson's stunning shots of the West's mountains, plains, deserts, rivers, and canyons seemed as powerful and compelling for nineteenth-century viewers as images of distant planets and galaxies are for us today. Somehow the photograph makes real what we only dreamed.

Jackson's vast, enduring body of work is a tribute to his energy, resourcefulness and, most importantly, his abiding sense of wonder. Born April 4, 1843, he lived ninety-nine years—just one year short of a century. Throughout his long, productive life, he maintained a spirited enthusiasm for the West and the great outdoors. His commitment was never more evident than in his struggle to capture an image in the high country of the Colorado Rockies in August of 1873.

That summer, when the muddy trail vanished and the struggling packhorses could not make it through the tangle of rain-soaked underbrush, fallen logs, and slick boulders, thirty-year-old Jackson and two assistants unloaded the bulky camera, fragile glass plates, and chemicals and shouldered the heavy equipment the rest of the way up the treacherous 13,000-foot slope.

They were in search of the impossible—a photograph of a legendary mountain. Rumor said that in certain seasons and wind conditions, an enormous cleft in the mountain's side would fill with snow and create a perfect, glimmering white cross. "No man we talked with had ever seen the Mountain of the Holy Cross," Jackson wrote in his autobiography. "But everyone knew that somewhere in the far reaches of the Western highlands such a wonder might exist."

After trudging above the timberline, Jackson perched for three hours with his camera ready and his musty canvas tent wrapped around his shivering shoulders for warmth. Impatiently, he waited for the clouds

Jackson and eighteen-year-old assistant Charley Campbell perched with camera, gear, and developing tent on Table Mountain ledge west of the Tetons in Wyoming Territory in 1872.

05. MOUNTAIN of the HOLY CROSS.

to part. What little light there was began to dwindle with the setting sun. Forced to give up, he climbed down a few thousand feet. He and his assistants spent the night beside a blazing fire, "supperless, blanketless on a bare rocky mountain side." Soon after daylight on August 24, Jackson was determined to try again. "Climbing up to 13,000 feet upon an entirely empty stomach & after the fatiguing exertions of yesterday," he admitted, "was no fun."

This time his effort was rewarded. The clouds cleared. The sun shone. As rapidly as possible, his assistants set up the darkroom tent and with cupped hands gathered what little snowmelt they could from a large hollow rock to mix with the chemicals. Jackson had just enough time to sensitize the glass plates and take eight exposures before the galloping shadows and clouds returned and blocked his view again.

Jackson's photograph of the Mountain of the Holy Cross would be one of his most famous works. Reproduced in thousands of prints, hung on walls, viewed in books and magazines and as a three-dimensional

(facing page) Rugged country separated Jackson and his goal in the distance, the snow-covered Mount or Mountain of the Holy Cross.

THE ROCKY MOUNTAINS
SCENES ALONG THE LINE OF THE
DENVER AND RIO GRANDE RAILWAY.

This popular version of Mount of the Holy Cross was printed between 1881 and 1889 for the Rio Grande Railroad.

stereograph, this image meant many different things to different people. For some nineteenth-century Americans, the elusive mountain, finally captured in a photograph, served as concrete, black-and-white proof of the West's marvelous promise—a place for new dreams.

Jackson's photographs speak to the people of today differently than they did to the people of the nineteenth century. After all, what an image shows depends on how and where and when and by whom it is seen. What remains the same, however, is the sense of privileged view that his work provides—a sense of discovery. We have found a place we perhaps never knew existed.

THE AMERICAN WEST IN 1869

CHAPTER ONE

THE GREAT RESTLESSNESS

(The American) is always in the mood to move on,
always ready to start in the first steamer that comes
along from the place where he had just now landed....
—Michel Chevalier (1806–1879)
   Society, Manners and Politics of the United States;
   Being a Series of Letters on North America, 1839

In 1853, when William Henry Jackson was ten years old, his family had already pulled up stakes and moved six times—zigzagging back and forth from upstate New York to Georgia to New York to Virginia to Pennsylvania and back to New York again. There is little wonder then that one of Jackson's earliest childhood memories was about traveling.

In 1848, when he was five years old and his family had uprooted itself once more to move from Georgia back to New York, Jackson recalled a mysterious evening when his uncle carried him above deck on the stern-wheeler on the Chattahoochee River "to show me the palmettoes and the shining waters under the light of a great full moon."

As a result of so much moving, there was little opportunity for much formal schooling. Jackson never acquired more than a grade-school education. As for his artistic training, he was completely self-taught. His mother, a gifted watercolorist, offered hints when she had the time. "But time was something she could not squander on one child," Jackson later wrote, "with five to care for and a home to run."

(facing page)
Towering rocks seemed to dwarf traveling survey men and their equipment near Platte Cañon, Colorado, in 1870.

Dapper, seventeen-year-old Jackson, photographic artist and odd-job decorator in Troy, New York, posed in a straw hat. The year was 1860 and Lincoln had just been elected president.

Jackson, who would eventually have six younger brothers and sisters, turned to J. G. Chapman's *The American Drawing Book*, an instruction book in drawing figures and landscapes. "No single thing in my life, before or since that day, has ever been so important to me," Jackson said. He became an even more avid artist. Whenever his family moved from place to place, Jackson carried with him his numerous sketchbooks. "I can hardly remember the time when I didn't draw pictures."

A NATION IN MOTION

The Jacksons' restless moves were typical of many families and individuals during the years just before and after the Civil War—a time described by one historian as "the Great Restlessness." People all over the United States were increasingly moving in and out of villages and cities and farms from East to West and back again. Some were looking for better jobs. Others sought better land. This movement signaled an enormous change in the everyday lives of ordinary Americans. Previously, most people had seldom traveled far from the places where they were born. They had little contact with the outside world.

By the middle of the nineteenth century, the movement in and out of the West had become especially noticeable. By one estimate, Westerners at this time pulled up roots an average of four to five times as adults. How extensive was this movement? One historian says that although there was a total of 100,000 people living in Colorado Territory for varying periods between 1858 and 1870, there was rarely more than one-third that number in the territory at any one time.

Horace Greeley (1811–1872), editor of the New York *Tribune*, traveled west in 1859. He described first-hand for his readers the people he encountered in Denver, a newborn gold rush camp hastily built from cottonwood logs. "Among any ten whom you successively meet, there will be natives of New England, New York, Pennsylvania, Virginia or Georgia, Ohio or Indiana, Kentucky or Missouri, France, Germany, and perhaps Ireland," he wrote. "You cannot enter a circle of a dozen persons of whom at least three will not have spent some years in California, two or three have made claims and built cabins in Kansas and at least one spent a year in Texas."

Before the coming of the railroad, people traveled west by wagon, by stagecoach, and even on foot pushing one-wheeled carts. The Great Restlessness was fueled in part by the Homestead Act. In 1862, during the Civil War, Congress offered 160 acres of public domain land to any man or woman who was age twenty-one or older and head of a family and either a citizen or about to become a citizen of the United States. Homesteaders could obtain title to 160 acres if they paid a ten-dollar filing fee and lived on the land and improved it for five years.

Land speculating companies quickly got around the rules and bought up the best land as quickly as

School children and their teacher stood outside of the first schoolhouse in Grand Junction, Colorado, around 1882.

possible and sold it at a profit to farmers and ranchers. Between 1860 and 1890 only an estimated one-tenth of new farms settled were actually acquired under the Homestead Act.

THE HOPE OF THE WORLD: CHANGING VIEWS OF THE WEST

Jackson, like so many Americans, grew up hearing many different stories about the West. Which were true? Which were lies? Even ordinary descriptions did not seem to satisfy. "One wants new words in writing about these plains, and all the inland American West—the terms *far, large, vast,* &c, are insufficient," wrote sixty-year-old poet Walt Whitman (1819–1892) during his first visit to the West in 1879.

The West had been a bewildering place from the moment Congress officially purchased much of the land from France in 1803 for $15 million in the Louisiana Purchase. Americans weren't sure who or what might exist in the vast, uncharted place known simply as Louisiana—territory that stretched mysteriously beyond the Mississippi.

President Thomas Jefferson (1743–1826) had his own ideas about this boundless terrain. One of his visions was a spacious region where independent farmers and their families could farm their own land. When he sent Meriwether Lewis and William Clark and the Corps of Discovery to explore and map the region in 1804, he instructed them to observe "the face of the country, its' growth & vegetable productions." He wanted details about the soil's fertility, the kinds of trees, the course of waterways—anything that would be valuable information for future farmers.

(facing page)
Argentine Pass, 13,132 feet above sea level, was first used by hardy travelers with horse and wagons in 1872.

Jefferson was so convinced of the West's enormity, he predicted that it would take countless generations of Americans to settle it. He would have been shocked to find out that the West was crossed, explored, and homesteaded in only eighty-nine years—just one lifetime.

As years passed after the explorations by Lewis and Clark, what began as a steady trickle of Western

GRAY'S PEAK FROM ARGENTINE PASS

settlement turned into a torrent. Oregon's rich land and mild climate were promoted in the 1830s with fanciful tales about a place so marvelous, one settler claimed, "Pigs are running about under great acorn trees, round and fat, and already cooked." The discovery of gold in California in 1848 heralded a tidal wave of hopeful miners and settlers. For some who visited Oregon and California and reported their findings in letters and newspaper articles, the West seemed like Eden—a kind of paradise with gentle winters, rich soil, and plenty of rain.

Other settlers, miners, and explorers weren't so impressed. What struck them about the West were the unforgiving plains and deserts that had to be crossed to reach California and Oregon. Explorer Major Stephen H. Long (1784–1864), who struggled across the southwestern plains to the Rockies in 1820, labeled the flat expanse "the Great American Desert" on the map he later published. Long called it a "dreary plain, wholly unfit for cultivation"—a place with too little surface water, too few trees, and too much heat.

By the time the railroad linked New York and San Francisco in 1869, there would be two very different views about the value of the West. Some people claimed that the West had to remain untouched. "In God's wildness lies the hope of the world," exhorted naturalist and writer John Muir (1838–1914). Others saw the West's value as a garden that could only be improved with settlement.

As settlement began to surge, a new third philosophy became popular. This time the key word was *transformation*. The Great American Desert could be made into Eden, promoters said, as soon as settlers moved out and farmed the place. What were people waiting for? "Rain follows the plow," a railroad pamphleteer declared, claiming that scientific evidence actually demonstrated that settlement changed and improved the climate. Even though the idea was far-fetched, Western small-town businessmen and other boosters seemed delighted to believe the idea.

For most European-Americans, spanning and settling the continent was a demonstration of divinely inspired progress, an idea that originally came across the Atlantic on the *Mayflower* when the country was first settled. These enthusiasts often quoted the Bible, stating: "Be fruitful and multiply and fill the earth and subdue it." Manifest Destiny, they declared, meant that it was not only Americans' right, it was their God-given duty to conquer nature and civilize Indians and anyone else who happened to thwart "Progress."

Of course, native people already living in the West had their own ideas about the landscape. To them, the West was home. Their religious philosophies and way of life were inextricably bound up in their view of the Western environment—not a place to subdue but a place full of mysteries of which they were a part.

When William Henry Jackson began working in the West as a photographer, his background, beliefs, and experience would color what he saw. They all had an impact on what he recorded for others with his camera. His challenge was to create images that captured the landscape's power and grandeur while giving his viewers a story they could understand. At every step along the way of creating his work, he was undoubtedly aware of the many often conflicting facts and fancies about the West that had been circulating in paintings, books, and speeches for generations.

Cowboys paused to have their photograph taken during a cattle round-up, perhaps in eastern Colorado in the 1880s.

013834. SILVERTON, COLORADO.

013834. SILVERTON, COLORADO.

CHAPTER TWO

THE TIMES AND THE PEOPLE

Go west, young man, and grow up with the country!
—adapted by Horace Greeley (1811–1872)
New York *Tribune*, 1865, from article that
originally appeared in *Terre Haute Express*, 1851

(below) Twenty-year-old Jackson's leather-bound pocket notebook from 1862 included sketches and jottings about his enlistment.

All his life William Henry Jackson was a tireless chronicler—first with a pen and then with a camera. For nearly eighty years he kept a diary, which was often nothing more than a small, palm-sized notebook tucked inside his pocket. His sketches, doodles, and "jottings," as he called them, reveal not only his observations of the world around him, but also his dreams and fears.

On August 2, 1862, when the Civil War had entered its second bloody year and President Abraham Lincoln seemed ready to draft troops to serve in the Union Army, nineteen-year-old Jackson laconically confessed: "Better to enlist voluntarily than to be dragged in as a conscript [draftee]... Nothing would be more degrading."

Like so many young men of his generation, Jackson had high hopes that soldiering might give him a chance to see the larger world beyond the small, sleepy town of Rutland, Vermont, where he worked as a retouching artist in a photography studio. The first thing he did after signing up with the Twelfth Regiment of the Second Vermont Brigade was to hurry off to the local dry goods store and buy one little rubber inkstand, a portfolio, 125 sheets of paper, and one stick of India ink to take with him to record what he saw in glorious battle.

(facing page) Local legend claimed that Silverton, Colorado, received its name when a mine operator bragged, "We may not have gold here, but we have silver by the ton." This image was taken sometime after 1880.

Private Jackson was relieved of ordinary fatigue duty so that he could roam and sketch such scenes as this one called "Winter Quarters."

During Jackson's nine-month stint as a private, he endured endless practice drills, bad food, blisters, soggy tents, mud, dust, and snakes. At the same time, he enjoyed the praise of his colonel for sketches he'd made of the company, the barracks, and the countryside. While stationed in Washington, D.C., he saw real art for the first time. William H. Powell's (1823–1879) enormous twelve-by-eighteen-foot landscape *Discovery of the Mississippi River by De Soto* hung in the rotunda of the unfinished Capitol. Jackson called this "a fine picture full of life and sunshine." At the Smithsonian he hungrily inspected everything from portraits of famous Indian chiefs to stuffed eagles. It all must have seemed terribly exciting.

When Jackson returned home to Troy, New York, one fine day in July 1863, he secretly hoped for a hero's welcome, even though, he later admitted, he had spent "the best part of a year at the front without firing once at the enemy." While no parade greeted Jackson, his family was thrilled to see him safe and sound again.

AMERICA AFTER THE WAR: "A NEW AND DIFFERENT WORLD"

Other soldiers weren't as lucky as Jackson.

When the Civil War finally ended in 1865, more than 620,000 soldiers had lost their lives—more fatalities than in all the nation's other wars combined, up to and including direct American involvement in the Vietnam War (1965–1975). Bombed buildings stood abandoned. Countryside lay smoking and scarred. Habits and hopes and ways of looking at life changed forever. Four million slaves were now freed, but the question still left unanswered was how whites and blacks would live together.

Some Americans found life after the war strange and confusing. "It was as if I had suddenly died and waked up in an entirely new & different world," confided Southerner Edward Porter Alexander (1835–1910) in his diary a few days after the surrender. "There are no words to tell how forlorn & blank the future looked to me."

Other Americans embraced the "new & different world," barely taking time to pause before plunging headlong into the raging, get-rich-quick race to rebuild. Cities like New York and Chicago boomed with the clang and roar of industrialization and growth. More than 10 million immigrants arrived in America between 1860 and 1890, the majority from northern Europe. Nearly 80 percent of these new arrivals settled in cities in the East and Midwest. Between 1870 and 1890, the population of New York City, the biggest city in America, skyrocketed from 1,478,000 to 2,507,000. Meanwhile, Chicago's population more than tripled—from 300,000 in 1870 to more than a million in 1890. American writer Mark Twain (1835–1910), who had worked as a steamboat pilot, miner, newspaperman, and performer, dubbed this time period the Gilded Age, an era bursting with "drive and push and rush and struggle."

New factories sprang up. New technology was invented and improved. Between 1870 and 1890, everything from steam boilers, electric lights, and elevators to telephones, telegraphs, and typewriters were introduced. New machinery in the workplace and home changed the lives of ordinary Americans.

At the same time, mechanical devices revolutionized the way farmers worked. Affordable new inventions such as wind-operated water pumps, barbed wire for "cow tight" fences, and steam-powered combines and twine binders to speed harvesting were promoted nationwide. The discovery of drought-resistant wheat seed and new milling techniques opened up crop possibilities, especially in the West where rainfall was so uncertain. The results were remarkable. American production of wheat boosted from 211 million bushels in 1867 to 599 million bushels in 1900. Fifteen bushels of wheat took an estimated thirty-five hours of labor to produce in 1840. By 1900 the same amount of wheat could be produced in just fifteen hours—slashing the labor time by more than half.

1869: "Hear that Lonesome Whistle Blow"

In 1869 most of America's forty million inhabitants still lived on farms or in small towns with populations of less than 2,500 people. In the next twenty years, thousands of men, women, and children would move into larger cities to seek work in factories. As cities increased in size, more and more Americans had to get accustomed to riding in streetcars; eating packaged, processed foods; and wearing factory-made clothing. They had to adjust to the crash and thud of heavy machinery in factories and the stench of smoke and soot from factory smokestacks and railroad stations.

Americans in small and big cities worked twelve-hour days, six days a week, without pensions, social security, or benefits of unemployment insurance if they were laid off. In 1870, one out of every three industrial workers was foreign-born. Recent immigrants, who mostly huddled in crowded, disease-infested tenements in Eastern cities, made up more than half the factory workforce by 1890. They lived in cramped, filthy rooms without plumbing. Native languages, foods, and lifestyles flourished in their crowded urban neighborhoods. By 1890 New York City would claim to be home to half as many Italians as lived in Naples, half as many Germans as in Hamburg, twice as many Irish as in Dublin, and two and a half as many Jews as in Warsaw.

Meanwhile, John D. Rockefeller (1839–1937) amassed millions in oil, while Andrew Carnegie (1835–1919) cashed in on steel manufacturing. Gustavus Swift (1839–1903) made his fortune in meat packing; John Pierpont Morgan (1837–1913) in railroads and finance. The wealthy of the Gilded Age spent incredible sums on yachts, private railroad cars, rare books, and famous paintings. They built themselves opulent fifty-six-room vacation "cottages" by the seashore and vied for attention to see who could entertain more lavishly. One millionaire held a fancy-dress banquet for other rich mens' pet dogs—

complete with linen, china, and fricassee of bones and shredded dog biscuits. Another hosted a gourmet meal for all his friends on horseback.

In spite of the huge chasm between the living conditions of the rich and the poor, the Gilded Age was a time of optimism. Opportunity seemed to be just around the corner for anyone with the right "luck and pluck." After all, hadn't Carnegie, a Scotsman, come to the United States dirt-poor in 1848? Through boundless ambition and hard work, newspapers reported, Carnegie made his first million by the time he was forty-eight years old. Stories of self-made millionaires made popular copy in newspapers and dime novels—just the encouragement Americans needed to believe that they, too, might one day be fabulously wealthy.

Nowhere was this national optimism more evident than in the celebration of the most amazing accomplishment of all: the completion of the transcontinental railroad. Begun in 1863 and finished in 1869, this stretch of 1,775 miles of track from Omaha, Nebraska, to Sacramento, California, was a remarkable engineering feat. It crossed deserts, blasted through mountains, and spanned rivers and canyons with daring tunnels and switchbacks and bridges. The train made possible for the first time travel from New York to San Francisco in just eight or ten days—a trip that had taken nearly five months overland by wagon or stagecoach and six months by sea around Cape Horn of South America.

The last spike was driven on May 10, 1869, in a ceremony on the windswept sagebrush plains of Utah. There, at a place called Promontory Point, Irish workers from the Union Pacific Railroad racing west met Chinese laborers from the Central Pacific Railroad racing east. A telegraphed message to cities across the country relayed news of the final spike blow. From Massachusetts to California, crowds gathered and cheered. Flags waved. Church bells rang. Cannons boomed. Fireworks exploded.

The United States, which had been divided North and South during one of the

Windswept Promontory Point in Box Elder County, Utah, marked the spot where track layers hammered the last rail in place for the transcontinental railroad.

most bloody struggles of all time, finally had something to celebrate: the connection of East and West. Cut in half now, the West lay waiting, as promising as a piece of split, ripe fruit. Here was a place to shed old identities and past failures. Here was a place to start fresh.

The West became one of the biggest land grabs of all times for the railroad companies. For every mile of track laid, Congress gave the Union Pacific and the Central Pacific 6,400 acres, or ten square miles, of federal land on either side of the track. In addition, each railroad received $16,000 for every mile laid across level prairie, $32,000 across plateaus, and $48,000 across mountains. The Union Pacific would eventually pirate a total of 19,000 square miles of land—more acreage than in the states of Massachusetts, Vermont, and Rhode Island combined. The land became a lucrative source of railroad income as it was sold to farmers.

Railroad agents fanned out across Europe, distributing handbills and encouraging various immigrant groups to come to America with fabulous claims. "Ho for the West! The truth will out!" declared a Burlington and Missouri River Railroad agent. "The best farming and stock raising country in the world!" The railroad had, in effect, become a "private colonizer."

With the transcontinental railroad complete, businessmen and politicians were certain that the West would be a new place to raise crops and cattle to feed the growing number of workers east of the Mississippi. The West's natural resources—lumber, coal, and newly discovered mineral bonanzas of gold and silver—would pour east while the finished goods—everything from factory-made shoes to steel plows and machines—would pour west.

In an era when the most highly skilled laborers in America earned less than $100 per month, a one-way first-class fare in the poshest Pullman Palace Car in 1869 was $100, plus $29 per day for a sleeping berth between Omaha and Sacramento. Second-class passengers paid $75; immigrants had a special rate of $40 to sit on hard board seats in crowded "Zulu cars," Western slang used to describe the cheapest available train accommodations.

THE GREAT MIGRATION

The year 1869 marked the beginning of the greatest migrations in American history. Over the next twenty years, the population of the land west of the Mississippi would skyrocket from seven million to sixteen million. Not everyone welcomed this growing mass of newcomers, however. In 1869, an estimated 444,000 American Indians were living in the West, as they had for generations before the arrival of white men. These native people stood to lose everything in the invasion.

With the coming of the railroad, buffalo herds and game disappeared. As settlers fenced more ranches and plowed more farms, open lands began to shrink. Miners, who burrowed into the hills and mountains in search of wealth, were quickly followed by belching, noisy smelters and stamping mills used in refining operations. The inevitable conflict between native people and white invaders during these years became a desperate last stand that would weave itself into both the heroic and tragic stories of the West.

Georgetown, Colorado, boomed after the first gold strike in 1859.

Taken in Echo Canyon 1869 —

W H Jackson. Photographer
Hayden Survey 1872

Jackson inspected a glass plate
outside his crude darkroom tent in
Echo Canyon, Utah, in 1869. The
handwriting on the photograph is
thought to be that of artist W. H.
Holmes, who served on the 1872
Hayden survey with Jackson.

CHAPTER THREE

IN SEARCH OF HIS FORTUNE

The thing that really got me was the railroad. Here was something truly earth-shaking, and, whether or not there had been a dime in it for me, sooner or later I would have been out on the grade with my cameras.
—William Henry Jackson
   Time Exposure, 1940

One month after the transcontinental railroad was finished, on blistering June 29, 1869, William Henry Jackson climbed aboard the Union Pacific train in the windy, raw town of Cheyenne, Wyoming Territory. He was twenty-six years old, 160 pounds, five feet nine inches tall, and "neatly assembled like an otter," a friend remembered. "He had the endurance of a bobcat and the easy balance and spring of a bighorn sheep." Jackson's eyes were pale blue, his hair brown and unruly. He wore a shapeless felt slouch hat and kept his pant legs tucked into the tops of his worn knee-high boots. His face was deeply tanned. His hands were calloused and stained.

No one on the train that day would have guessed that back in Rutland, Vermont, just three years earlier, Jackson had sported spotless plug hats, rich ties, and brocaded waistcoats. When he wasn't courting the town beauty, playing the flute, or racing fancy carriages around town with the other young bloods of his social set, he worked for twenty-five dollars a week in a photographic gallery. Indoors, day after day, his job as a retouching artist required only enough muscle to sit on a stool and dab a photograph with a brush or pencil. When his romance abruptly ended, he slipped out of town at night, too humiliated to say good-bye to his friends. "When you had a broken heart, or too much ambition for your own good—there was always the West," Jackson later admitted.

After arriving in the West in 1866 and working as a bullwhacker on the Oregon Trail and herding wild horses from California to Nebraska for a year, in 1869 he considered himself a hard-boiled Westerner. He looked no different from the other restless, wispy-bearded, eager-eyed young men on the train that day who were also seeking their fortunes. Some were fellow ex-Union soldiers. Others were former Rebel soldiers who had fled destroyed homes and dreams in the South.

All were on the move, riding elbow to elbow with families of hopeful "honyockers"—farmers from Michigan and Illinois and Ohio—and immigrants just off the boat from Germany, Russia, Scandinavia, and the British Isles. Chinese and ex-slaves and Mexicans traveled on the Union Pacific, as did American Indians, whose claim to the land the train had destroyed. The babble of languages must have been confusing and noisy.

Of course, Jackson probably wasn't paying much attention to the other passengers as he boarded the train that day in 1869. He would have been too busy keeping his eye on the baggage handlers as they cursed and recklessly heaved the precious, dead-weight crate marked "Jackson Brothers Photography" onto the train. Jackson winced but did not protest. He couldn't. He and his energetic assistant, twenty-three-year-old Arundel C. Hull (1846–1908), plus all of their equipment, were spending the summer riding the rails free of charge. The railroad encouraged photographers like Jackson, who wasn't on the Union Pacific payroll but whose work would publicize routes and encourage passenger travel. Always savvy about dealing with people, Jackson made it a point, he said, to "keep on the right side of all the various (train) employees."

Neither Jackson nor Hull could be sure how they'd reach their next destination. Sometimes they clambered onto handcars, other times they hailed freight and gravel trains. Occasionally they would even toss all their belongings onto the cowcatcher on the front of an enormous belching steam engine and hang on for dear life.

This was an exhilarating summer for Jackson—his first independent photographic expedition. He had left Mollie Greer, his bride of less than one month, back in the comfort of civilization in Ohio with her parents while he set off. His brother Ed had been instructed to manage the photo studio they jointly owned in Omaha, Nebraska. "Portrait photography never had any charms for me," Jackson confessed. He and Hull were on the prowl, Jackson wrote, "in quest of the picturesque and marvelous."

His ambitious summer plan was to take his camera and equipment on the new Union Pacific line and photograph "views" of scenery along the way and sell them in the little railroad towns that had sprung up along the tracks. Without a horse or wagon, Jackson and the resourceful Hull had to haul everything by hand once they clambered off the train. "That first outfit," Jackson later wrote, "was a very unwieldy, bungling affair."

Jackson and Hull were completely dependent on the train's schedule. They could only move on if another engine happened by. If they ran out of chemical supplies, they had to wait for days for special-order deliveries on the next stagecoach or train through town. To save money, they camped along the tracks. If they were lucky, they would share cans of peaches and sardines and feast on chunks of bread and cheese—all washed down with thick, sluggish river water "sweetened with lemon sugar." When funds ran low, they would eat stale crackers.

Terrific winds often whipsawed their tent. "Dust would sift through everywhere and was a great inconvenience," Jackson wrote in his diary on one particularly stifling day. "Cockroaches and ants...would hide and crawl in our ears and mouth while we were sleeping." In spite of these hardships, Jackson scribbled breathless diary entries about his encounters with the Western landscape. "The scenery of Echo and Weber [Cañons] appeared magnificent and will keep me continually perplexed when I come to select views."

The Great Iron Horse, as the railroad was originally called by the Indians, transformed Jackson's career. In it, he found a subject to photograph, a patron, and the means of transportation into difficult

terrain. Jackson knew this was his chance to make a name for himself. He was determined to learn how to master photographic exposures in the brilliant, thin Western light and how to position his camera to capture the perplexing, magnificent scenery where every vista seemed enormous and overwhelming. Little did he know that he was also gaining firsthand experience about how to sell his work.

By June 29, Jackson had been on the rails for almost a month, and he was almost out of money. Would he have anything to show for himself when his trip was finished? As the train picked up speed across the Wyoming plains, cinders flew in the open train car windows. Absentmindedly, Jackson thumbed through a stack of his photos. He did not notice the approaching teenage "train butch," a boy who sold passengers everything from newspapers and cigars to joke books and razor-thin ham sandwiches.

In 1871 Jackson tilted his camera lens upward to Yellowstone's Tower Falls to create an image of rocky walls that seem about to topple on the viewer.

The ambitious Union Pacific employee studied Jackson's views over his shoulder. He must have known a commercial success when he saw one, because moments later he made a business proposition. His suggestion would forever change Jackson's way of looking at his own work.

"Had a talk about pictures with a train boy," Jackson recorded briefly in his diary. "Sold him the remainder of my Indians [pictures brought along as samples]. Said he should want a thousand stereos of scenery about Weber Cañon the first thing [to sell as souvenirs to tourists on the line]." Then Jackson added one more practical detail: "Slept in our seats at night."

This conversation started Jackson thinking. Maybe there were more photo customers out there than he'd realized. He could sell to tourists, certainly. But what about people trapped in cities and small towns miles away? Maybe they hungered for views of the wide open spaces of the West, too. That day he wrote to his brother in Omaha and demanded that he contact distributors on the East Coast who sold three-dimensional photographs called stereographs.

Two months later, on August 23, while photographing small railroad settlements in eastern Utah, Jackson went into a local post office and discovered a letter from his brother. Ed had enclosed the response from Edward Anthony in New York, who ordered "10,000 of our [Union Pacific] views." With this order, Jackson's work suddenly gained national recognition. His photos would be part of the Anthony series entitled *Views Along the Union Pacific Railway*.

This would be Jackson's first big break.

PHOTOGRAPHY: "WRITING WITH LIGHT"

In 1869, when Jackson was first earnestly "in quest of the picturesque and marvelous," photography in America was only thirty years old. Although still in its primitive phase of development and riddled with possibilities for mistakes, photography (when it succeeded) turned out to be one of the most powerful and convincing media for capturing the West. The reason? Americans at the time were convinced that photographs, unlike paintings, could not lie. People were so sure of this that they called photographers "operators," to show how little people like Jackson had to do with the way an image came out. Operators were only doing the mechanics of making the photo. Nature did everything else.

Nineteenth-century Americans regarded photography as nothing short of a miracle when it arrived in this country from France in 1839. The earliest images, called daguerreotypes after French inventor Louis-Jacques-Mandé Daguerre (1789–1851), were astonishing.

These palm-sized, one-of-a-kind representations were so fragile that they had to be enclosed in glass inside a hinged case of leather or velvet. Because the daguerreotype was created using metal etched with chemicals, the viewer had to hold the image to the light and tilt it just so to see all the details. Philip Hone (1780–1851), a fifty-nine-year-old New Yorker and lifelong diarist, was confounded when he viewed the French daguerreotypes on display at a friend's gallery. He used a magnifying glass to examine the images. "Every object, however minute," he wrote on December 4, 1839, "is a perfect transcript of the thing itself: the hair on the human head, the gravel on the roadside, the texture of a silk curtain, or the shadow of a smaller leaf reflected upon a wall."

This daguerreotype of an unidentified little girl and her doll was taken some time between 1842 and 1860 by an unknown camera "operator."

The invention was such a terrific hit, some people predicted that it would spell the end of painting. Everyone wanted to have their daguerreotype taken, even if it meant sitting completely still for almost five minutes while hooked to a hidden metal neck brace to keep them from moving and blurring the image. This discomfort may have been one reason why many of the people in early portraits appeared so solemn. Smiling naturally—and not moving—would have been a daunting challenge.

Daguerreotype amateurs of all kinds quickly took up the craft. Watch repairers, dentists, even blacksmiths were known to offer the service as a sideline. In 1860, 3,154 men and women listed their profession as "photographic operators" in the U.S. census. By 1890, that number would reach 20,040.

The Breakthrough: Multiple Images from One Negative

The next big step was the invention of a process that would allow many images to be easily and cheaply created from one exposure. In 1851, an Englishman introduced the collodion or "wet-plate" process that used chemicals and glass plates to create negatives. Collodion is a thick, syrupy liquid made by dissolving nitrated cotton in a mixture of alcohol and ether.

Developing a Negative Using the Wet-Plate Process

Step One: Working in complete darkness, the photographer coated a glass plate with collodion, then dipped the plate into silver nitrate to make the glass light-sensitive.

Step Two: Before the chemicals dried, he had to slip the plate into a special shield that kept out light.

Step Three: He rushed out of the darkness and placed the shielded plate inside the camera.

Step Four: By opening the lens cap, he exposed the plate for five seconds to twenty minutes, depending on available light.

Step Five: Next, he scurried back to the darkroom to develop the glass negative before its chemical coating hardened and lost sensitivity.

Step Six: The plate was fixed with a solution of hyposulfite of soda.

American photographers adopted the European-style portable dark tent shown in A History and Handbook of Photography, *(1877). An assistant holds the next shielded glass plate while the photographer focuses the camera. Inside the tent are chemicals used to create wet-plate negatives.*

Step Seven: The plate was washed thoroughly with water.
Step Eight: The plate was allowed to dry completely.
Step Nine: The plate was varnished to preserve the image.

Making Albumen (or egg white) Prints
Multiple copies of one image were created by using special sensitized paper coated with albumen.
Step One: The glass plate was placed on the paper and exposed to the sun.
Step Two: Then the paper was toned or colored by submerging it in a metallic bath solution that gave the print the characteristic red-brown earth color.
Step Three: The print was fixed or made permanent in a solution of hyposulfite of soda.
Step Four: The print was rinsed with water, air dried, then glued to cardboard using wheat paste.

The process required a great deal of eye-hand coordination. Muscles often came in handy, too. Because the print could only be as big as the negative, camera and glass sizes became large, heavy, and unwieldy in order to create large prints—some of which used glass that was two feet wide.

STEREOSCOPE: TAKING THE ARMCHAIR TRAVELER TO THE ENDS OF THE EARTH

When the collodion process was invented, a new kind of photograph became increasingly popular. This was the stereoscopic view, a specially created photograph that if examined through a special device gave the viewer the shocking sense of seeing a scene in three dimensions.

To make stereoscopic views, a special double camera with two horizontal lenses two and one-half inches apart was used. Each lens recorded the image as seen by each eye. The resulting prints were pasted on a piece of cardboard with an accompanying caption identifying the scene. One New York stereograph company that began business in 1859 issued more than ten thousand different titles over the next twenty years, ranging from dizzying shots of Niagara Falls to sheep herders in Ireland.

A stereoscope

In 1860, a dozen views cost $1.50, and a stereoscope viewer ranged in price from just $0.62 to $12.00. Eventually, the price of owning a stereoscope and a set of stereo views became so low that nearly anyone could afford this popular form of entertainment. As Herman Vogel, a photochemistry teacher, declared in 1883: "I think there is no parlor in America where there is not a stereoscope."

The real power of the stereoscope was its breathtaking ability to transport a viewer from his armchair to some faraway mountain. A twenty-four-year-old Illinois schoolteacher named Frances Willard (1839–1898), who would one day become a champion of temperance and women's suffrage, first saw stereographs in 1863 while visiting a friend in Pennsylvania. As soon as she peered into the stereoscope, she became so entranced that she lost track of time and could not hear or see anything else going on around her. "I seemed shut in a different world," she wrote in her diary. "I was looking at actual representations—photographs—of scenes far off; —of which I had visions sometimes; —of which I had read with delight; —which in my prayers I had often asked to see."

Cards such as this one with photographs of Niagara Falls fit into a stereoscope and give viewers the sense of seeing in three dimensions.

Trestlework stretched over Echo Canyon in Summit County, Utah, in 1869.

CHAPTER FOUR
"SURMOUNTING EVERY BARRIER": CAPTURING IMAGES OF THE WEST

I see over my own continent the Pacific Railroad
surmounting every barrier,
I see continual trains of cars winding along
the Platte carrying freight and passengers,
I hear the locomotives rushing and roaring,
and the shrill steam whistle,
I hear the echoes reverberate through the
grandest scenery in the world.
—Walt Whitman (1819–1892)
"Passage to India," 1871

Technological improvements in photography boomed at the same time the settlement of the West boomed. And riding the crest of this wave of enthusiasm and change was Jackson himself, who had the remarkable good fortune of being in the right place at the right time. In 1868, he had located his first photo studio in thriving Omaha, the jumping-off place for the Union Pacific.

In 1869 Jackson created a trademark woodcut drawing to advertise Jackson Brothers Photography in the Omaha *City Directory*. The dramatic drawing, which also later appeared on the back of some of Jackson's photographs of the Union Pacific route, shows a train chugging around the bend of a mountain

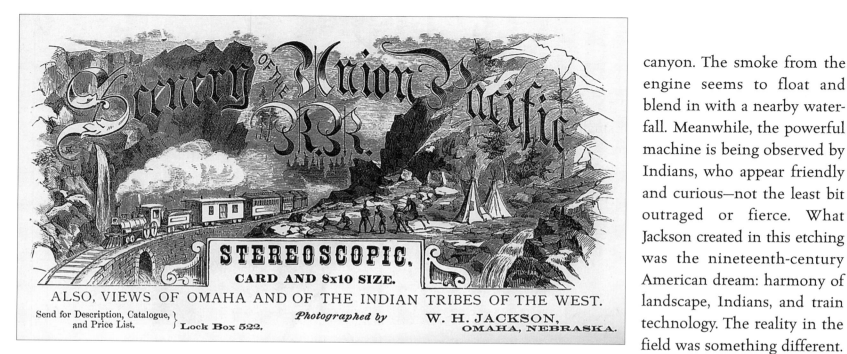

canyon. The smoke from the engine seems to float and blend in with a nearby waterfall. Meanwhile, the powerful machine is being observed by Indians, who appear friendly and curious—not the least bit outraged or fierce. What Jackson created in this etching was the nineteenth-century American dream: harmony of landscape, Indians, and train technology. The reality in the field was something different. Photographing the railroad in the Western landscape peopled by often hostile tribes would prove to be a much more challenging endeavor.

American East Coast artists, who had been influenced by European art and training, typically created paintings of pretty little trains chugging through sleepy hillsides. This approach clearly would not work with a camera in the West. Jackson and other photographers like him were determined to show the power of the train and its relationship with the strange, often larger-than-life landscape of the West.

In 1869, Jackson was still learning how to use the camera's expressive capability. Contrary to what many people at the time thought, photographers were not mere operators. They made many choices that had an important impact on how their images ultimately looked. They could choose between lenses that would make space seem shallow and compressed or enormous. Choosing different light and times of day created different skies in photographs. Different angles of light revealed different illuminations of rock. Canyon walls could seem harsh or deep, depending on the light. By tilting the camera up or down or to the side, the image might make viewers feel superior to a scene or small and vulnerable—as if a rock slide might crush them at any minute.

Because Jackson had no formal art training, he had fewer preconceptions about how the West was *supposed* to look. This made it easier for him to start fresh. He just jumped in and started shooting. He made plenty of mistakes and tried his best to learn from them.

"This was a period of great experimentation for me," he wrote. "The art of timing exposures was still so uncertain that you prayed every time the lens was uncapped, and no picture was a safe bet until the plate had been developed."

Not only did he have to achieve mastery over the technical challenges of photography, he had to figure out what to photograph. This was also accomplished through trial and error. He discovered that what worked aesthetically for him and what his audiences seemed to appreciate sometimes matched, sometimes did not. Eventually he found that the most effective images were the ones that showed the power of the train *and* the power of the landscape. These were photos that revealed the blasting of sides of mountains, the gritty infinity of the tracks, the heroic engineering of what looked like impossibly fragile railroad trestles stretching across sheer drops of canyons. American viewers wanted to see an even match. And they wanted to see someone in the picture, maybe a person leaning beside the track or part of a crew scrambling up a rocky hillside. A human figure gave the photograph scale, a way for the viewer to understand just how big that rock in the photo was. As big as a house? No, bigger.

Jackson studied the railroad shots taken by A. J. Russell (1829–1902), the unofficial photographer of

Ambitious, twenty-seven-year-old Jackson is shown here in an 1870 photograph.

GLACIER POINT. YOSEMITE

the Union Pacific. He tried imitating some of Russell's work, not always with success. Eventually he found his own style. He discovered that he could use the railroad tracks themselves as a kind of horizontal ladder that looked as if it went on and on forever into the distance. He often made the vast expanse of sky an overpowering element in his photographs. Sometimes he positioned his camera to show how a rocky cliff towered over the tracks in a threatening way.

He took physical risks to get the shots he wanted. He scrambled down into canyons so that he could position his camera looking up at railroad cars that skirted the bridges above him. He

"Working in a fully equipped studio was hazardous enough," Jackson wrote of his early years. "Going at it in the open meant labor, patience, and the moral stamina." This undated photograph was taken at Glacier Point, Yosemite, California.

clambered out onto railroad trestles high over raging rivers. He took pictures along the Union Pacific line of subjects as diverse as Devil's Slide and the Thousand Mile Tree. What he saw inspired him deeply. "The bold promontories and the peculiar isolated turrets of...sandstone...with quiet lovely valleys occurring between," he wrote in his diary, "possess in themselves all the varied attractions any artist could wish for." He was continuously learning and relearning what the Western landscape meant.

PHOTOGRAPHS OF THE WEST TRAVEL EAST: "THE REAL THING ITSELF"

By the early 1840s, as soon as the process to create daguerreotypes became widely circulated, cameras were lugged across rivers, plains, deserts, and mountains by hardy, enterprising photographers. The earliest daguerreotypes in the West were undoubtedly those of gold miners in California who had arrived as early as 1849. Miners with tents, blankets, and frying pans stood stiffly in hopeful poses for loved ones back home.

Unfortunately, few of the very earliest attempts at recording the Western landscape have survived because of accidents, Indian attacks, or technological blunders. In 1851, Robert Vance exhibited 300 daguerreotypes of California. These were among the first photographs of the West to reach audiences in New York. These pictures of California seemed so incredible that they were advertised with a warning: "These views are no exaggerated and high colored sketches, got up to produce effect, but are...the stereotyped impression of *the real thing itself.*"

In the early 1860s, California landscape photographers like C. E. Watkins (1829–1916) used a stereoscopic camera to record the enormous redwoods near San Francisco. He photographed spectacular Yosemite Valley, which was also captured in mammoth-sized glass plates by Eadweard J. Muybridge (1830–1904).

Ten years later, a wildly popular form of entertainment for Easterners hungering for Western views was the "illuminated lecture." In New York City, "Professor" Stephen James Sedgwick thrilled auditoriums packed with enthusiastic audiences who came to hear him talk about enlarged photographs illuminated on the wall with a special "magic lantern" operated with limelight. With each change in photo, Sedgwick would describe for his viewers a panoramic journey across the West on the Union Pacific. Some of the photos Sedgwick used to narrate his popular program throughout the 1870s had been taken by Jackson.

PHOTOGRAPHS OF THE EAST GO WEST

At the same time exotic Western photographs were being taken and sent to eager Eastern audiences, familiar, unadorned photographs were being carried West by homesteaders and miners as precious mementos of relatives and friends left behind. This two-way traffic shows how important photographs had become for ordinary Americans. Since the very beginning of Western migration, photographic portraits or "likenesses" helped bridge the separation between people who most likely would never see each other again.

During the Scott family's trip west from Illinois to Oregon Territory in 1852, the mother and youngest child died from cholera. The survivors, who included six sisters and two brothers, continued the five-month journey. Eleven-year-old Harriet Scott, nicknamed Duck, took along her beloved grandfather's daguerreotype. When the family finally arrived, she wrote to him, "We have got your likeness and it does me a great deal of good to look at it. It looks very naturael [sic] indeed."

The importance of these images becomes even more clear in a letter written in December 1880 by a homesick miner snowed in at a mining camp in Colorado. "Why have I not gotten any picture of my loved ones?" he wrote plaintively to his relatives back in Virginia.

For many settlers, photographs brought from the East had special significance in their new lives in the West. In 1864, E. J. Dickson and his family homesteaded in Montana. Their cabin, which measured only sixteen by twenty feet, had chinked log walls painted with clay. The dirt floor was beaten hard and smooth. In spite of cramped, crude conditions, the family made a special effort to convert a flour barrel into a kind of parlor center table, "whereon reposed the family Bible," he wrote, "and the photograph album with their white lace covers."

Travelers gazed at scenery from Phantom Curve in the Colorado Rockies. Jackson took the photograph between 1881 and 1892 to tempt tourists to take the train.

CHAPTER FIVE
AMERICANS TAKE TO THE RAILS

Nothing helps scenery like ham and eggs.
—Mark Twain (1835–1910)
Roughing It, 1861

Naturally, the Union Pacific and other railroads were delighted to have photographers like William Henry Jackson taking photographs along the line for passengers and people back East who might one day consider coming West on the train. Early on, the railroads organized excursions for reporters and photographers.

One promotional tour through Kansas in August 1868 included an observant lawyer named John H. Putnam, who rode from Topeka to Monument and back again—approximately 700 miles—in forty-five hours. A crowd of photographers and two hundred pleasure seekers made the trip from Topeka to the end of the line, compliments of the railroad. They were furnished with "refreshments, consisting of Ice Cream, Lemonade, Sherry [*sic*] Cobbler, Mint Juleps, Wine, etc." Needless to say, after a few hours in the blistering heat and wind and dust, the passengers began to have "a withered, squeezed lemon appearance," wrote Putnam in a letter to his brother. Boredom ended when a troupe of hired Indians raced around the train "performing" a mock battle and attack.

Once the promotional excitement of the new railroad died down, passengers traveling cross-country soon discovered that the West looked different from a train than it had from a wagon or a stagecoach or the back of a horse. Hurtling along at the top speed of twenty-five miles per hour meant that details just outside the train window vanished in a blur. Jackson's photographs took on new meaning for travelers.

By purchasing his images, they could make sure they saw and kept forever the scenery that sped by so quickly they sometimes barely made out more than a distant outline.

In 1869 few towns interrupted the vast Western landscape spanned by the new railroad. Travelers spent days in what appeared to be a gigantic void. Space seemed to expand. "We were at sea—there is no other adequate expression—on the plains of Nebraska," wrote twenty-nine-year-old Scottish writer Robert Louis Stevenson (1850–1894) about his cross-country train trip in 1879. "It was a world almost without a feature; an empty sky, an empty earth; front and back." The train seemed to toil "over this infinity like a snail."

Twelve hours west of Kansas City on a train bound for San Francisco, a traveler from Finland noted in her journal, "A peculiar, sharp smell of hay, dust and cattle strikes one. Some pleasant smells are interfused with it, too, just like the fragrance of dried spices."

West of Promontory Point in what is now Utah, a kind of dust plagued travelers. "A coating of alkali dust gives [the Great American Desert] the appearance of a snow-covered plain," commented H. F. Rae, an English journalist traveling across America in 1869. "But snow is far less intolerable than alkali…shoe-leather is burned by it as by quick-lime. The minute particles which float in the air irritate the lungs and throat."

The wind was the passengers' constant companion across the plains. One traveler climbed out of a stopped train car to collect buffalo bone souvenirs along the track and was instantly knocked flat by the howling breeze. "Such a wind! Shrieking round the cars and converting the telegraph poles into the chords of a ghostly harp," wrote Frank Leslie(1821–1880), publisher of the popular *Frank Leslie's Illustrated Newspaper*. For five months beginning in April 1877, Leslie made a splashy cross-country trip in a private Pullman train car supplied with oysters, caviar, and champagne. Accompanying him were his wife, Miriam, and her nasty Skye terrier, two close friends, and half a dozen staff writers and artists. His series about his trip ran in his weekly newspaper for two years. Many of the illustrations for his newspaper were engravings made by copying photos by such photographers as Jackson.

First-class passengers soon discovered, however, that even the poshest accommodations did not shield them from fickle Western weather. Rudyard Kipling (1865–1936), a twenty-four-year-old Englishman fresh from travels in India, journeyed from San Francisco to Chicago in 1889 in a Pullman car. He complained that a "profusion of nickel-plating, plush and damask does not compensate for closeness and dust...that long coffin-car was by no means ventilated, and we were a gummy, grimy crew who sat there."

While dozing fitfully in the stifling heat on the rolling plains of eastern Colorado, Kipling was suddenly awakened by intense cold and what sounded like "the drumming of a hundred drums. The train had stopped," he wrote. "Far as the eye could range the land was white under two feet of hail—each hailstone as big as the top of a sherry glass. I saw a young colt by the side of the track standing with his poor little fluffy back to the pitiless pelting. He was pounded to death."

Plenty of dangers lurked along the train route, from loose rails and washouts to buffalo on the tracks. Drunk cowboys in some little railroad towns had the habit of shooting for fun at bright trains passing through at night. Engineers solved the problem of blasted windows by temporarily turning off all the lights.

In the High Sierras and parts of the Rockies, heavy snow or avalanches might wipe out whole sections of track. Railroad workers built wooden tunnels called snowsheds over the track to help keep the way clear. Kipling did not find these hastily constructed structures the least bit reassuring. He called them "horrible caverns of rude timbering." Leslie had a different view of them. He and his wife found them an irritating torment because "they shut out the very most interesting and ardently desired points of scenery."

The train's ascent up the mountains was slow and nerve-racking. "The first section of the cars crawled a quarter of a mile ahead of us, the track snaked and looped behind, and there was a black drop to the left," Kipling wrote. "So we went up and up and up till the thin air grew thinner and the *chunk-chunk-chunk* of the labouring locomotive was answered by the oppressed beating of the exhausted heart."

Eventually the train gasped its way to the highest point—nearly 11,000 feet above sea level. From there, everything was straight downhill. The train dropped 2,200 feet in thirteen miles.

"It was not so much the grinding of the brakes along the train track, or the sight of the three curves of track apparently miles below us, or even the vision of a goods train apparently just under our wheels, or even the tunnels, that made me reflect," Kipling said; "it was the trestles over which we crawled—trestles something over a hundred feet high and looking like a collection of match sticks...groaning, shivering trestles."

Kipling was especially unimpressed by American construction of tunnels in the Rockies. He decided that human life was "of small account out here." He felt relieved to escape unharmed through two terrifying miles inside Stampede Tunnel, which he described as nothing more than the gallery

This 1882 photograph was taken in the dizzying Cañon of the Rio de Las Animas in Colorado.

*Further down the
line, the trestle bridge
groaned as the train
came to a stop over
the waters of the Rio
de Las Animas. The
engine towered next
to a rather foolhardy
man standing on the
tracks in this undated
photo.*

of a mine shored with timber and lighted with electric lamps. "Black darkness would be preferable," he said, "for the lamps just reveal the rough cutting of the rocks, and that is very rough indeed. The train crawls through, brakes down, and you can hear the water and little bits of stone falling on the roof of the car. Then you pray, pray fervently, and the air gets stiller and stiller, and you dare not take your unwilling eyes off the timber shoring, lest a prop should fall, for lack of your moral support."

Occasionally, crashes did occur. Rae wrote about a collision in Nevada when some oxen wandered across the tracks. "A sudden shock roused all from their slumbers," he recalled. "Many [passengers] were greatly frightened, but no one was seriously hurt. A severe shaking was the only result of what proved to be a collision with a herd of cattle. The engine and tender had been thrown off the rails. Two oxen were crushed to death." Rae and the other passengers waited eight hours for a replacement engine sent after a telegraphed message was finally relayed.

IMMIGRANTS HEAD WEST

While Rae, Kipling, and the Leslies were making the train journey to collect information for a book or series of newspaper and magazine articles, thousands of other train travelers at the time were setting off with less grandiose schemes. They were heading west to start their lives over again.

No one was more aware of this than Robert Louis Stevenson, who traveled third-class and described himself as an "amateur immigrant." "All the states of the North had sent out a fugitive to cross the plains with me," he wrote. "From Virginia, from Pennsylvania, from New York, from far western Iowa and Kansas, from Maine that borders on the Canadas, and from the Canadas themselves—some one or two were fleeing in quest of a better land and better wages. The talk in the train...ran upon hard times, short commons and hope that moves ever westward."

One of the most disheartening sights was crowded trains returning east. "Whenever we met them," wrote westward-bound Stevenson, "the passengers ran on the platform [at the back of the train car] and cried to us through the windows in a kind of wailing chorus, to 'Come back.' On the plains of Nebraska and in the mountains of Wyoming, it was still the same cry, and dismal to my heart."

Those who managed to escape the cities were the lucky ones, the ones with money. By the 1870s immigrants were needed by the millions to keep the western railroads afloat financially. The railroads required a constant stream of customers to help pay for new locomotive equipment, construction of expanding track routes, and worker salaries. Throughout Europe, agents canvassed small villages and big cities alike looking for "hardy, sturdy farmers with money" who could afford to come to America, take the train west and buy land. Jackson's photographs, which had been copied into engravings, were used in Europe to illustrate brochures and posters.

In the 1870s immigrants paid $26.80 to ride from New York to Council Bluffs packed in a railroad car with eighty-nine other people. Until a bridge was built in 1872 across the Missouri River, travelers had to board a ferry to Omaha. Here they made their way to the Union Pacific station. Immigrant families crammed the Zulu cars with all their belongings—everything from trunks to featherbeds. For the next ten days of their trip from Omaha to San Francisco, they slept on hard board seats and cooked their own meals on the one small, coal-burning stove in each car. If they had any spare cash, they bought expensive stale food at small railroad towns.

By the early 1880s the railroads realized that settlement success rates were higher among immigrants who came with their neighbors and could help each other. Entire European villages were encouraged to emigrate together—especially if residents had plenty of money. Yet in spite of their ability to buy a train ticket and purchase land, new arrivals often met with ridicule.

Miriam Leslie sniffed critically when she encountered immigrants bound for the Black Hills of Dakota Territory. "The strangest and most motley people," she said. "Men in alligator boots and loose overcoats made of blankets and wagon rugs, with wild, unkempt hair and beards and bright resolute eyes, almost all well-looking, but strange as denizens of another world...women looked tired and sad and queerly dressed in gowns that must have been old on their grandmothers, and with handkerchiefs tied over their heads in place of hats."

Nothing matched the racial prejudice experienced by groups of Chinese, American Indians, and African Americans, who were herded into separate cars when they traveled by train. During the 1870s and 1880s nearly 120,000 Chinese lived in the West, mostly single men who worked on the railroads and in the mines. They tried to make enough money to return home with their savings. The striking appearance and unusual clothing of the hardworking Chinese made them an easy target for racial slurs. They spoke a strange language and wore basket hats, flopping blue clothes, sandals, and pigtails. They carried their supplies on bamboo poles. But worst of all, they were willing to work for less money than white laborers. This made them threats.

Extreme violence erupted in places like Los Angeles in 1871, when twenty-three emigrants were hanged, shot, or stabbed in a two-day riot. In 1877, depression gripped the West and the rest of the country. Many people accused the Chinese of taking jobs from Americans. Anti-Chinese violence broke out in towns and mines in Wyoming, Idaho, Colorado, and Washington. Lynchings, lootings, boycotts of Chinese businesses, and eventual mass expulsion culminated in 1882 when the Chinese were the first group to be refused entry into the United States with the passage of the Chinese Exclusion Act of 1882. In 1881, 40,000 Chinese had been allowed into the country. The year after the Chinese Exclusion Act, that number dropped to only twenty-three.

Prejudice was seldom far from the surface during encounters between whites and Asian emigrants on the trains. While in what is now Elko, Nevada, in 1871, Rae saw four or five Chinese women and a few children making their way through the crowd on the train platform of the station. "China women are seldom seen in public," he wrote. "One or two China men entered the train here. Among them was a merchant who had amassed a fortune, who spoke English fluently, and who conversed intelligently on most subjects. He was not allowed a seat in the best cars, but was condemned to occupy a place in the emigrants' cars. All his money could not conquer the prejudice against his tribe."

Stevenson noted that American Indians were allowed to ride the train for free but were often subjected to cruel treatment once they boarded. "I saw no wild or independent Indian," he wrote; "indeed, I hear that such avoid the neighborhood of the train but now and again at way stations, a husband and a wife and a few children, disgracefully dressed out with the sweepings of civilization, came forth and stared upon the emigrants. The silent stoicism of their appearance, would have touched any thinking creature, but my fellow-passengers danced and jested around them with a truly Cockney baseness. I was ashamed."

Three travelers climbed out onto the engine's "cow catcher" and another sat on the roof as the engine idled in Colorado's narrow Royal Gorge, also known as the Grand Canyon of the Arkansas.

CHAPTER SIX
THE HAYDEN EXPEDITIONS

Never has my faith in the grand future that awaits the entire
West been so strong as it is at the present time.
—Dr. Ferdinand Vandeveer Hayden (1829–1887)
United States Geological and Geographic Survey,
Annual Report, 1870

A major turning point in William Henry Jackson's life came quite by accident while he and Arundel Hull were taking photographs along the Union Pacific tracks in the summer of 1869. On a hot, dusty afternoon in June in the raw, wild "Hell on Wheels" railroad town of Cheyenne, Wyoming Territory, Jackson bumped into Dr. Ferdinand Vandeveer Hayden, famous geologist, scientist, and Western booster. Jackson was delivering a finished photo order to Madame Cleveland's establishment—a kind of saloon, gambling hall, and brothel—just as Hayden was arriving. Hayden, who had met Jackson a year earlier in more polite society back in Nebraska, seemed distinctly embarrassed when he was recognized. "Was much surprised to see Dr. Hayden come in with some military friends," Jackson wrote in his diary. "He acted like a cat in a strange garret."

This chance encounter may have helped jog Hayden's memory about Jackson and his camera a year later in Omaha, when he decided to visit Jackson in his studio and view the images Jackson had taken the previous summer. Hayden was impressed. He was also desperate. He needed a photographer to go with him on an expedition that had just received funding from Congress to observe, collect, report, and

(facing page) Artist S. R. Gifford suggested to Jackson that he could create a sense of drama in his sweeping landscapes by positioning people like actors in the scene. Here, Gifford sketched the Chugwater River in Platte County, Wyoming, during the 1870 expedition.

illustrate the West. In 1870, the secretary of the interior had instructed Hayden to "secure as full material as possible for the illustration of your final report, such as sketches, photographs, & etc." Hayden had already hired several painters and artists, but he knew a photographer would provide the accuracy and visual impact his expedition needed to be a complete success.

Would Jackson be willing to pack and leave in one week to go on an expense-paid trip that would take him away from his Omaha studio, his wife, and his business for three months—without pay?

A more cautious man might have calculated the risks and consulted with his wife. Not Jackson. Without pausing, he said yes, packed his bags, and left Mollie in charge of the studio. Jackson never regretted his decision. "For me," he later wrote, "the expedition was priceless—it gave me a career." By hitching his future to Hayden's star, Jackson entered a whole new world of possibilities as a photographer. Since 1868, Hayden had been building a solid reputation by leading scientific surveys west of the Missouri River. These expeditions were undertaken to give railroad experts, businessmen, and military and government officials information about the terrain, Indians, and resources. This was data that could be used to create new businesses, farms, ranches, mines, and railroads.

Dr. Ferdinand Vandeveer Hayden is shown in this undated photo, hunting geology specimens with his trusty rock hammer.

Hayden's background was in medicine, but his passions were more eclectic and varied than that. He enthusiastically embraced geology, paleontology, biology, zoology—anything and everything that had to do with minerals and landforms, animals and plants in the West. On one early expedition, the Lakota named the high-strung collector of geology specimens "The Man Who Picks Up Stones Running." A group of hostiles reportedly found him wandering by himself in a remote area. He carried no gun—just a bag of rocks. The Indians left him alone because they thought he was only a harmless, crazy man.

Hayden's genius was his imagination, energy, and ability to convince Congress to raise necessary funds to pay for the expeditions and publish the results so widely that the information would be available to the general public. As a result, many schoolchildren in the 1870s and 1880s viewed the natural wonders of the West using stereopticon slides and photographs taken on Hayden's expeditions. Other Americans visited museums where collections had been amassed by Hayden's staff.

THE 1870 EXPEDITION

As part of the 1870 expedition—Hayden's biggest and most expensive to date—Jackson would be allowed to keep his negatives. By traveling with the government-supported and -protected expedition, he was able to visit and take pictures of places no one had ever photographed before. He worked with respected experts in the fields of botany, anthropology, meteorology, and zoology. He created images alongside famous landscape painters who directly influenced his work. The expeditions were the culmination of Jackson's education.

Jackson eagerly soaked up details about everything he could, from rock strata and dinosaur fossils to American Indian tribes and cloud formations. "For every mile on the map we covered between two and three on the ground—up mountainside, down stream bed, across country—to gather rock specimens, to survey and map, and to paint and photograph," he wrote. He met the physical challenges of expedition life without complaint. A fellow camper described him as "companionable." On the expedition he was good natured and helpful, quick to joke or lend a hand. He loved the outdoor life and the spirited company of other expedition members. Most of all, he found the work "engrossing and satisfying."

The routine for his first expedition would be very like that which he would follow on subsequent trips:

Every day we had an informal conference around the camp fire and then we would set about our work individually, or in groups of two or three. One little division might be assigned to calculate the flow volume of a stream; another would be given the task of sounding a lake; several other men might investigate the geology of the region or hunt fossils; [Sanford R.] Gifford, [Henry W.] Elliot, and I would go off to record our respective impressions of a striking landmark....Dr. Hayden had the rare compound faculty that enabled him not only to select able assistants but to get all of them to pull together...he made every man feel that each little individual side trip was vital to the whole...

On July 31, 1870, Jackson took the train for Cheyenne and would not return home until November 1. The expedition rolled out with twenty men; four heavy wagons to carry supplies of food, bedding, and scientific equipment; and two lighter Army ambulances to use for side trips. Each man rode on his own

Surveyors Ada D. Wilson (left) and Franklin Rhoda record data about nearby ranges from Sultan Mountain in La Plata County, Colorado, during the 1874 expedition.

horse or mule. A cook provided all the meals. Jackson's assistant John H. Beaman, who also served as staff meteorologist, helped load and unload equipment. Compared to Jackson's grueling 1869 railroad trip, this venture must have seemed luxurious indeed.

The expedition traveled along the Oregon Trail, what had become the Union Pacific route. No photos were taken of the railroad on this expedition. Jackson instead recorded landmarks such as Independence Rock. Hayden worked closely with Jackson, telling him what to shoot yet allowing him on occasion to range into the wilderness in search of views. Jackson made 150 whole-plate views using his new five-by-eight-inch camera. He also created more than 150 stereo views. He worked with expe-

"Killed by Indians" was the inscription on the lonely grave marker of a soldier near the campsite of the 1874 expedition on the Sweetwater River in Wyoming. Gifford is pictured with a gun.

dition painter Sanford R. Gifford, who showed him how to look at a landscape using more traditional composition methods.

Jackson experimented with people in his photographs. Rather than posing them only to show scale, he made them actors in the scene itself. Sometimes he had them gazing thoughtfully out over the distant mountain or nearby lake. Unlike his earlier, grittier railroad pictures where Nature seemed to challenge the heroic deeds of men, these images showed people as welcome visitors, "tiny but not threatened, utterly respectful," one historian remarked. Nature appeared ready to be explored.

At the same time, Jackson's photos revealed the heroic expedition at work—clambering over rocks, scaling cliffs, surveying mountains. Hayden certainly appreciated these shots, because they demonstrated to Congress and other people in the East how difficult his expedition's job was.

When their work was completed, Jackson and the rest of the expedition team went to Denver. After a brief visit with his wife in Omaha, Jackson left home and headed out on the road again. He personally oversaw the transport of all his glass negatives, which were shipped to Washington, D.C. There he was given a studio and an office. He had to work quickly. Hayden was eager to publish the expedition's report, which included 500 pages of text—ten times bigger than the year before. Jackson's photographs were distributed after the report was published on January 1, 1871.

Hayden was so pleased with Jackson's work, he offered him a year-round salary. Congress must have been equally awed. After viewing the photographs and studying the report, Congress authorized $40,000 for the next year's expedition—twice that of the previous year.

During the next seven years, from 1871 until 1878, Jackson served as Hayden's chief photographer on seven different expeditions that ranged all over the West. In the course of this work, Jackson took thousands of photographs. The rest of Hayden's team amassed a vast archive of information. Every year Hayden issued an annual report hundreds of pages long.

A veritable deluge of information about the West was produced and made available to the public. This

Hayden wanted Jackson's pictures to tell the heroic story of the rough and ready life of the expedition. This 1871 camp study includes (left to right) Jackson; A. C. Peale, mineralogist; C. S. Turnbull, secretary, and teenager George B. Dixon, assistant.

was an astonishing body of work that reflected the Gilded Age's enthusiasm for science and its optimism about the conquest, settlement, and exploitation of the West. Over the years, Jackson's photographs continued to be regarded as accurate and useful in conveying information about the land and the plants and rocks. As Hayden himself said, the medium of photography was "the nearest approach to a truthful delineation of nature." Hayden also appreciated the fact that Jackson's work was beautiful, a quality that helped assure continued congressional support and public attention.

Landscape painter Thomas Moran gazed into the dazzling multicolored pools and formations of Mammoth Hot Springs on Gardiner River during the 1871 Yellowstone expedition.

CHAPTER SEVEN
NATURAL CURIOSITIES

Each new turn in our zig zag trail opening up new vistas that rendered our admiration speechless...
—William Henry Jackson
   Diary, August 28, 1874, near Stoney Pass, elevation 13,000 feet, Colorado Territory

1871–1872: Wonders of Yellowstone

For nearly forty years, mountain men had told stories about an amazing place in the Teton Mountains of Wyoming Territory where water boiled in wild-colored springs, hidden canyons revealed bizarre rock formations, and geysers exploded from deep underground. In 1826 a group of explorers wandered into the region. One of those men, Daniel T. Potts, wrote a letter home to Philadelphia describing the wonders:

On the South border of this Lake, is a number of hot and boiling springs, some of water and others of most beautiful fine clay, resembling a mush pot, and throwing particles to the immense height of from twenty to thirty feet. The clay is of a white, and of a pink color, and the water appears fathomless, as it appears to be entirely hollow underneath.

Over the years the stories grew with even wilder embellishments. Were they true? No one knew for certain. With an eye for publicity possibilities, Hayden decided that the Yellowstone River valley was the perfect place for the 1871 expedition. Hayden was no fool. He knew that the Northern Pacific Railroad was considering running a new line through the Yellowstone region to take advantage of what explorer Nathaniel Pitt Langford (1832–1911) described as "the highest display of artificial culture, amid the greatest wonders of Nature that the world affords." It seemed only a matter of time before tourists piled out of trains, eager to see the sights.

No photographs had yet been taken of the Yellowstone region. Hayden also knew that the amazing geology of the region was yet to be fully investigated. He quickly pulled together supplies and left from Salt Lake City with thirty-four men and seven wagons on June 11, 1871.

Joining Jackson and the rest of the artistic and photographic team was a new member, the renowned

The 1871–1872 Hayden Expeditions' pack train is pictured on the trail between the Yellowstone and East Fork Rivers in Wyoming.

landscape painter Thomas Moran (1837–1926). Moran had never in his life been camping in the Rockies or ridden a horse. "He was 34 years old at the time, of slight and frail physique," Jackson remembered. Moran, who would become Jackson's lifelong friend, "did not seem to be the kind to endure the strenuous life of the wilderness. But he was wiry and active in getting about and keenly enthusiastic." While getting used to riding a horse, Moran tucked a pillow atop his saddle.

Moran had left England with six brothers and sisters when he was seven years old. The family went to Philadelphia, where his father, a textile worker, found work. Moran eventually made many trips to Europe to study romantic paintings and poetry. Both Moran and Jackson came from working-class backgrounds and were largely self-taught. Both shared an enthusiasm for the Western landscape.

Jackson's original photograph of Moran was probably heavily retouched in pencil by Moran.

They influenced each other in many ways. While Moran's approach was more dramatic and romantic, Jackson's photographs revealed a new, bold directness after they began working together. Moran helped Jackson hunt down the best spots to set up his two new large cameras, which produced 6 1/2-by-9-inch and 8-by-10-inch negatives. Jackson's shots in turn helped Moran, who used the images when he returned home to complete enormous, dizzying, full-color landscapes on canvas.

The expedition's first stop in Yellowstone was the Mammoth Hot Springs, a boiling "spa." They were surprised to discover the springs were being used by a group of "invalids," who soaked in the hot water while planning to create a toll road to the area they would rename McQuirk's Medicinal Springs.

No matter. Jackson set up his camera and went to work. As the expedition approached the isolated interior of the Yellowstone region, the rock formations and cliffs became increasingly strange, like something

The stunning 1871 image of the Grand Canyon of the Yellowstone was taken from the east side of the river one mile beneath the falls looking down.

from another planet. Unlike the photographs from the previous year, Jackson did not include survey members—except for one shot, *Crater of the Castle Geyser*. This photograph revealed a tiny figure crawling up a steaming geyser mouth—perhaps a geologist risking his life to gather scientific information.

When Jackson and the rest of the exhausted expedition returned to Washington, D.C., in October 1871, they began the feverish activity of printing photographs and publishing their findings. Although two other photographers had been in the Yellowstone region that season, fate would have it that only Jackson's photographs were published. T. J. Hines took photographs on an earlier expedition to Yellowstone that year. Unfortunately, he returned to his hometown of Chicago just in time to have all his work destroyed by the disastrous Chicago Fire of 1871. J. Crissman of Bozeman, Montana, accompanied Hayden's expedition as a guest photographer. His camera was perched on the edge of the Yellowstone Canyon when a strong gust of wind sent it tumbling into the depths. The camera was never recovered.

Hayden was in a race with time. That fall Congress was considering setting aside Yellowstone's two million acres to create the first large-scale national park. A variety of interests had already expressed support: banking and railroad companies wanted to use the park to boost tourism. Government-backed explorers wanted to keep the wonders preserved. Other Western boosters living in the area saw the park as a way to increase their own land's values.

Jackson's spectacular photographs, along with the other amazing specimens brought back from the expedition, were put on display for congressmen to view. The photographs were proof that the earlier wild stories were indeed true. There really *were* mud geysers, erupting craters, bubbling hot springs, spectacular waterfalls, and colorful canyons.

In 1872, Congress was convinced of two things. First, the Yellowstone region was *only* good for tourism. (There didn't seem much hope for agriculture or mining.) Second, general traffic would increase dramatically if the park were made into "a specimen of virgin land and sublime spectacle," tourist businesses would boom, and the surrounding area would be quickly populated.

Yellowstone was officially made into a national

The Yellowstone expeditions witnessed the unpredictable 250-foot Giant Geyser eruption at the Upper Geyser Basin, one of the tallest.

park on March 1, 1872, in a ceremonial signing by President Ulysses S. Grant (1850–1912). Congress was so impressed by Hayden's work that he was given $75,000 to return to Yellowstone to finish his exploration. Congress even set aside $10,000 for Hayden's artists to create engraved illustrations made from Jackson's photographs. These engravings would be published in the next year's report.

Although his photographs were powerful persuaders in convincing congressmen to set aside Yellowstone as a national park, Jackson never let the success go to his head. "Pictures were essential to the fulfillment of the doctor's plan for publicizing this Survey," Jackson wrote, "but the basic purpose was always exploration. I cannot be too careful in emphasizing the fact that in this and all the following expeditions I was seldom more than a side show in a great circus."

While away in Washington, D.C., printing his Yellowstone negatives for the congressional exhibit, Jackson met with personal tragedy. He had sent his pregnant wife to live temporarily with his parents in Nyack, New York. He planned to join her as soon as he could. Before he could return, Mollie died in child-

Some of the most striking sights Jackson discovered on the 1871 expedition were Yellowstone River canyons, valleys, and waterfalls.

birth in February 1872. Their first and only child, a daughter, survived just a short time. "These are matters," Jackson confided seventy-one years later, "about which, even now, I can write no more."

Soon after his wife and daughter's deaths, Jackson was back in Washington, D.C., planning for the next expedition. He had sold the Omaha studio in the fall of 1871. In the summer of 1872, Jackson returned with Hayden to Yellowstone to reexplore the region. This time he was part of a team of sixty-one men divided into two parties. He and Moran would again attempt to capture some of the sights they had visited earlier, including a remarkable shot of Old Faithful erupting. Throughout this survey, Jackson used an eleven-by-fourteen-inch camera—his biggest yet.

It would not be until 1878, the last year of Hayden's expeditions, that Jackson returned to

On his return to Yellowstone in 1878, Jackson made many fascinating five-by-eight inch glass negatives of such sights as Fountain Geyser on the Lower Firehole River.

Yellowstone. By this time, congressional support for Hayden's work had begun to wane. Hayden gathered his team and with his last season's funding of $75,000 set out to try to show that he could do some very scientific exploration. Unfortunately, by this time tourists rocketed around the countryside in fast buggies and on horseback to sightsee around the geysers and relax in the hot springs. As early as 1874, the secretary of the interior wrote to President Grant to demand "protection of this great natural wonder from the vandalism of curiosity-hunters."

Jackson did not write in his diary about the changes he saw in Yellowstone in 1878. If he had, however, he probably would have agreed with Rudyard Kipling, who visited the famous Beehive and Turban Geysers a few years later. Kipling was appalled to discover tourists "chipping the cones to pieces, or worse still, making the geysers sick." As a joke, some visitors had dumped soft soap by the barrelful down geysers to see what would happen.

Jackson's 1878 photographs of Yellowstone showed members of the expedition looking into some of the formations that Kipling described. They are not as dashing and brave as earlier expedition poses. "They seem exhausted," one historian wrote, "bowed down by some responsibility or weight."

1873–1878: WONDERS OF COLORADO

The photographs Jackson took in Colorado from 1873 to 1878 were among some of his best—in spite of accidents, failures, and disappointments. Throughout this period, he continually experimented with new film, larger camera formats—his biggest yet was a camera that used 20-by-24-inch plates—so enormous that it had to be transported on its own mule. This camera narrowly avoided disaster when the mule rolled off a mountain trail and lodged between two trees.

With each successive trip, Hayden gave Jackson more responsibility and freedom. By 1872 he had his own cook, assistants, pack mules, and a delightful sense of power as he set out down the trail. As he later explained, "I felt like a general in command of an army. This was *my* expedition." He wasn't far from wrong. In spite of whatever economic calamities seemed to be falling upon the rest of America during the Panic of 1873 and later during the Depression of 1877, Jackson was the commander of his own kingdom.

It was also during these years that he remarried. His new wife, Emilie Painter, was the daughter of a Quaker Indian agent he had first met while in Nebraska in 1868. "Even knowing the worst—that I was a traveling man—she accepted my proposal and set the wedding for October." Their simple wedding took place in October 1873, just twenty months after

In 1874, a year after her marriage, Emilie Painter Jackson was photographed atop a pony on the Omaha Reservation where her father was Indian agent. The other women and man are unknown.

his first wife died. Emilie, who was the niece of the governor of Colorado Territory, would assume a much more traditional, socially ambitious role than Mollie, who had been Jackson's business partner and studio manager during his long absences. Emilie would never enter the arena of the photo business. Her world was the more traditional Victorian ideal of the female "realm of the home."

Jackson and his new bride rented rooms in a Washington, D.C. boarding house close to United States Geological Survey headquarters. Hayden had ambitious plans for the upcoming survey of Colorado in 1874. Although anything but unexplored, Colorado had not been reliably mapped. The government was interested in detailed topographical information that described how high mountains rose and valleys fell. Mining concerns were interested in finding out as much as possible about mineral resources. Since the discovery of gold in 1858 and of silver in 1864, Colorado crawled with miners and prospectors. Where might the next strike be found?

79. FALLS AT FOOT OF ROUND TOP MTN.

The summer of 1873 took the expedition into the central Rockies. The expedition was divided into six separate divisions to cover as much ground as possible.

Interestingly enough, while climbing 14,255-foot Longs Peak in September 1873, part of the expedition took along a thirty-one-year-old woman named Anna E. Dickinson (1842–1932), who provided some interesting insights into the heroics of the expedition in her book *A Ragged Register*. With each passing year, Hayden and his team seemed to have risen in national stature as courageous explorers. Dickinson described Hayden as "tall, slender, with soft brown hair and blue eyes—certainly not traveling on his muscle; all nervous intensity and feeling, a perfect enthusiast in his work, eager of face and voice, full of magnetism." As for the other expedition members, she wrote with breathy eagerness:

> I looked at...all the little party, with ardent curiosity and admiration, braving rain, snow, sleet, hail, hunger, thirst, exposure, bitter nights, snowy climbs, [and] dangers of death...

Beginning in 1873, however, one of the challenges that the expedition faced was the growing Colorado population. No longer in iso-

High in the Rockies, in the headwaters of the Colorado River, Jackson in 1874 recorded this waterfall at the foot of what he called Round Top Mountain (later known locally as Mount Baldy).

lated "sublime wilderness," Hayden and his men had to learn how to do their jobs while dealing with irate ranchers, incompetent local guides, unfriendly miners, and pesky tourists and health seekers. On one occasion Jackson could not cross a mountain lake because all available boats had been commandeered by "a great many pleasure seekers [who] find their way here, coming generally in their wagons and camping for a number of days at a time."

Ambitious early settlers sometimes set up toll roads on mountain passes, forcing travelers like Jackson and his assistants to pay "15 cts the animal." Jackson also noted with disgust the effects that mining operations were having on the Colorado environment. "[The Blue River] is anything but what its name indicates. A more turbid, yellow muddy stream I never saw," he wrote in his diary. "The extensive gulch mines about its source is the cause."

Much of what Jackson managed to photograph during his five expeditions in Colorado were pristine lakes and mountains—vast panoramas created by putting together two to six plates. In these panoramas, he made a point of avoiding showing any signs of settlement.

Jackson later reflected:

"Potato John," cook on the 1874 expedition, received his nickname because of his "passionate but futile attempt to boil some spuds soft enough to eat at an altitude of 12,000 feet."

When I came to Colorado I was about at my best, not only in the particular of photography required but also in the usages of camp life of travel in uncharted regions. When hard pressed for time, I have made a negative in fifteen minutes, from the time the first rope was thrown from the pack to the final repacking. Ordinarily, however, half an hour was little enough time to do the work well. Thirty-two good negatives is the largest number I ever made in one day.

FISHERMAN'S CABIN ON GRAND LAKE. 68.

In 1874 one of the few cabins to be found beside Grand Lake, 8,367 feet above sea level, was this crude fisherman's house.

Jackson had learned how to work quickly and efficiently. Yet he did not swerve from tackling physical challenges. To outsiders, however, his fervor may have seemed a bit strange. A local fisherman named Charles Wescott lived high in the back country near limpid, cold Grand Lake, 8,369 feet above sea level.

Jackson hired Wescott during the summer of 1874 to help carry equipment. "In Wescott's opinion, Jackson was a little 'tetched' to climb to the outlandish heights that he did," one local historian wrote, "much less lug all his 'traps,' as Jackson called his equipment."

On August 1, 1874, Jackson took pity on Wescott on the way down after a difficult fifteen-mile hike to photograph some waterfalls above Grand Lake. "[Wescott] got tuckered & I took his pack in mine," Jackson confided in his diary.

Undoubtedly, one of Jackson's most famous Colorado mountain pictures was that of the Mount of the Holy Cross, which was taken in 1873. This photograph would have a profound effect on American poet Henry Wadsworth Longfellow (1807–1882).

In 1879, almost eighteen years after the tragic death of Longfellow's first wife, the poet was sitting in his parlor looking at an illustrated book of Western scenery. He came upon a lithograph created from Jackson's photograph of the Mountain of the Holy Cross. That night Longfellow's glance fell upon a picture of his wife that hung in his bedroom. He was inspired to write the poem "The Cross of Snow":

There is a mountain in the distant West
That, sun-defying, in its deep ravines
Displays a cross of snow upon its side.

Snow-covered twin peaks of Gray (left) and Torrey rise more than 14,000 feet in height in Clear Creek County, Colorado. In 1873 a pass between the two peaks served as a lifeline between Georgetown and other mining camps.

Such is the cross I wear upon my breast,
These eighteen years, through all the changing scenes
And seasons, changeless since the day she died.

Longfellow hid the poem after he wrote it. The verse was not discovered until after he died in 1882.

Jackson converted a wagon into a traveling darkroom and ventured out into the Omaha Indian reservation in 1868 to take photographs. He had only a few months' camera experience when he took this image in front of the tepee where Chief Gi-He-Ga lived.

CHAPTER EIGHT

CLOSING IN: AMERICAN INDIANS IN THE WEST

For the European who came from a community of congestion and
confinement, the West was...wild, definitively wild. And it was inhabited
by a people who were to him altogether alien and inscrutable, who were
essentially dangerous and deceptive, often invisible, who were savage
and unholy—and who were perfectly at home.
—N. Scott Momaday, Kiowa writer (b. 1934)
  The West: An Illustrated History, 1996

It was fitting, perhaps, that one of Jackson's first views of buffalo in huge numbers occurred while he was traveling on a train. More than any single machine, the locomotive was responsible for the end of the buffalo. When the transcontinental track was finished, the great buffalo herds on the plains had been effectively cut in half. Ancient north-south migration patterns were destroyed. The railroad not only brought more people West to hunt, it provided a cheap, fast way to transport buffalo hides East.

As Jackson journeyed to Washington, D.C., on the Kansas Pacific in the fall of 1870, the train stopped unexpectedly. When Jackson looked out the window to see what was wrong, he spotted a mass of shaggy beasts making their way across the plains. "I would guess not less than half a million," he said. They were so closely packed together, they looked like a moving carpet. The sight made Jackson recall something he once heard an old plainsman say: "A man might have walked across the valley on their huddled backs as on a floor."

THE END OF THE BUFFALO

When white men first arrived in North America in the 1500s, an estimated seventy-five million buffalo roamed three million square miles of open prairie and grasslands. These enormous animals weighed close to two thousand pounds and stood six feet at the shoulder. By the time the Indians on the Great Plains were introduced to guns and horses by white traders, buffalo could at last be easily hunted.

Plains Indian religion, philosophy, and very survival depended on the buffalo. This remarkable creature was put to twenty-two different uses. Red Cloud, Lakota chief, recorded:

> His meat sustained life; it was cut in strips and dried, it was chopped up and packed in skins, its tallow and grease were preserved—all for winter use. Its bones afforded material for implements and weapons; its skull was preserved as great medicine; its hide furnished blankets, garments, boats, ropes, and a warm and portable house; its hoofs produced glue; its sinews were used for bowstrings and a most excellent substitute for twine.

The coming of the railroad spelled the end of the buffalo. While the Union Pacific railroad (later renamed Kansas Pacific) was being built in 1867, construction crews were fed buffalo meat provided by hunters like railroad employee William F. "Buffalo Bill" Cody (1846–1917). Cody reportedly killed 4,280 buffalo in just eighteen months. It was not unusual for a hunter with a good rifle to bring down 100 or 200 a day.

Many people believed the buffalo to be so numerous, there would always be plenty. In 1869, William D. Street, a settler in northwest Kansas, spotted a herd twenty miles wide, sixty miles long. He guessed there were "perhaps 100,000 or 100 million." Buffalo herds were so thick and numerous that when they forded rivers, they stopped steamboats midstream. When they crossed tracks, they halted train traffic.

Slaughter of buffalo began in earnest in the early 1870s, first on the southern plains and then on the northern plains. When Eastern manufacturers discovered ways to cheaply tan buffalo hides for shoe leather, carriage tops, and belts for machinery, buffalo killing became big business. Wholesale dealers in New York paid $16.50 for one first-class buffalo skin. In the first three months of 1872, 43,029 hides and 1.4 tons of buffalo meat were shipped east from Dodge City, Kansas. In the next two years in Dodge City alone, an estimated 3,158,730 buffalo were killed mostly by white hunters. (Of these, 405,000 were killed by Plains Indians.) Most of the carcasses were stripped of their hides. The meat was left to rot.

Shooting buffalo was viewed as great sport from a moving train. Sometimes when a herd

In 1870 a pile of buffalo, elk, deer, mountain sheep, and wolf skulls and bones in Albany County, Wyoming, revealed how abundant game once was on the plains.

was sighted, the train stopped. "Now the fun begins," wrote a traveler in Kansas in 1868. "Everybody runs out and commences shooting—Nothing hurt...I did not shoot...But I rushed out with the rest—yelled promiscuously—'Buffalo'—'Stop the train'—'Let me out.'"

Eventually, the destruction of the buffalo brought the Indians into "submission." They could live on reservations and receive rations or face starvation. "I think it would be wise," wrote General William T. Sherman (1820–1891), Western commander in charge of military operations, "to invite all the sportsmen of England and America [to the Republican River] this fall for a Grand Buffalo hunt, and make one grand sweep of them all."

Sherman's words would prove prophetic. By 1884, the buffalo would become nearly extinct. The last carload of robes and hides shipped came out of Dickinson, Dakota Territory—a measly collection of only 300.

FIRST ENCOUNTERS

In 1492, when Columbus first landed on the North American continent, an estimated population of between three million and ten million people inhabited North America. By the middle of the nineteenth century, that number had plummeted by nearly ninety percent. European diseases—smallpox, diphtheria, measles—took the most powerful toll on the native people, most of whom had no immunity to these diseases.

By 1868 only 360,000 Indians from west of the Mississippi were surviving. They shared an uneasy space with nearly 84,000 other Indians who had been uprooted earlier from their eastern woodland homes and swept west to reservations. The West was a volatile, changing place, where hunting territories often overlapped and caused conflict.

TRIBES OF THE WEST

It would be too simple to say that there was one giant wave of white migration that washed against a solid barrier of opposing Indians. What happened in the West was a wave that broke over a heap of scattered Indian groups that had been fighting one another for generations and would continue to fight one another to the day of their final conquest by whites.

The Indians of the West had always been culturally diverse, depending on where they had adapted and lived. The Kwakiutl of the Pacific Northwest traditionally fished and built their houses from planks of wood. Pueblo people of the dry mesas of New Mexico herded sheep, raised corn and beans, and built their houses with adobe in a continuous large village unit like an apartment house. On the plains the nomadic Crow disdained farming, made their living by hunting, and lived in buffalo-hide tepees that could be quickly and easily transported.

No label fits all Western Indians, except to say that in 1869 most raised crops, gathered wild edible foods, or hunted enough to survive—and little more. They were not interested in amassing individual wealth. They depended on simple technology, worshipped deities arising in nature, and strove for a balance in the natural world. The major tribes of the West spoke many different languages and had widely varying beliefs. All had had some contact with whites—an association that went back nearly 400 years with the coming of the first horses of Spanish explorers in the early 1500s and the first guns traded with the French and English around 1600.

On the 1874 expedition Jackson persuaded this Ute in full eagle feather headdress to pose on horseback at the Los Pinos Agency in Colorado.

Most of the Western tribes exalted in war and fought in ways to celebrate the individual. They all venerated their homelands and many practiced some sort of aggression against neighboring tribes. They were chronically in grudge matches and frequently committed acts of revenge. Among all Western tribes, land was viewed as a group possession and looked upon as something no one person could own. The "sale" of land, as the whites understood it, was a foreign concept to Indians and the source of much confusion and miscommunication with whites.

A FASCINATION BEGINS: JACKSON AND THE INDIANS

Jackson began observing Indians in 1868, his first year in Omaha. Native people were the subjects of some of the first photographs he took outside the confines of his studio. He would pack up his camera and go on the road for three or four days at a time, traveling 100 miles or more, to photograph Osages and Otoes who lived south of Omaha. To the west on the Platte River lived the Pawnees. North along the Missouri were the Winnebagoes and Omahas. "Those Indians would pose for me by the hour for small gifts of cash, or just for tobacco or a knife or an old waistcoat," Jackson wrote. "And I in turn was able to sell the pictures through local outlets and by way of dealers in the East."

Many of these early portraits were set up with help from the Indian agent Edward Painter, a dedicated doctor who would one day be Jackson's father-in-law. Painter's job was to help with "the moral uplift and education" of the Omaha Indians. Painter was in charge of a reservation, a place viewed as a kind of holding tank for Indians. The reservation was land that the government had promised the Indians as a place they could live and farm "like white people," while receiving free food and clothing payments and sending their children to white-run schools.

On the reservation, the Indian poses Jackson used were picturesque and designed to appeal to the

Eastern ideal of what a "good Indian" was supposed to be—either a noble, natural man now living on a reservation or an eager Indian convert hoping to learn how to farm and live in a house like a white man.

Jackson had rigged a traveling darkroom from a buggy fitted with a water tank and other essential gear. Eventually, after the local livestock stopped bolting when they saw his contraption come into sight, he was "welcomed equally," he wrote, "before the tepees of the Poncas and the earthen homes of the Pawnee." This may have been a bit of an exaggeration. Jackson himself admitted that some Indians considered photographers "bad medicine."

Jackson arrived on the Pawnee and Omaha Indian reservations in 1868, the same year the Fort Laramie Treaty was signed. This treaty had set aside the Great Sioux Reservation—all of present-day South Dakota west of the Missouri River, including the Black Hills—"for the absolute and undisturbed use and occupancy of the Sioux." For four years, the government said, the Indians would be provided with food and instruction in farming. In exchange, the Sioux had promised to give up traditional ways. They were to stop harassing railroad construction, molesting wagon trains and emigrants, and taking whites captive.

Chief Pe-ah (left) and other Ute leaders display peace medals from President Grant.

INDIANS OF THE WEST: 1869

After the signing of the Fort Laramie Treaty, Lakota Chief Red Cloud and his people had peacefully withdrawn in small groups to hunt buffalo in the Powder River country in what is now southern Montana. He was occasionally joined in hunting expeditions by several other famous warriors, including Crazy Horse, who remained an uncompromising foe of reservations.

On the southern plains, demoralized Kiowas and Comanches, Cheyenne and

Arapaho had retreated to reservations, following the Medicine Lodge Treaties. They had given up most of their land in Nebraska and Wyoming but soon found reservation life confining. The food was scant and poor although liquor was available for sale by white ranchers. Meanwhile white commercial hunting of buffalo destroyed remaining herds.

In southwestern New Mexico and Arizona, after years of raids on ranchers and miners from Rio Grande and Tucson and deep into Mexico, the Apaches had also been encouraged to try out the offers of an Indian agent. Weary of losing so many warriors and still having little to show for their efforts, they had been promised safety—food, clothing, blankets, and protection against white posses seeking scalps—if they would come to the government reservations and send their children to school. So far none of these offers had come to fruition.

In the Pacific Northwest, some Nez Percé, who were called "Christian and progressive" by their agent, had moved to a reservation in Idaho in 1855. Eight years later they were forced onto a smaller reservation when gold was discovered inside their first reservation's boundaries. Not all Nez Percé went along with the move. Chief Joseph, a famous leader, refused to live on the reservation. In 1869 he and a small band of followers lived in their beloved Wallowa Valley in northeastern Oregon. Each year agents tried to remove them. Each year Chief Joseph and his followers refused to leave.

This encampment at the Los Pinos Agency in La Plata County, Colorado, appears deserted in this 1874 photograph.

INDIANS OF THE WEST:
AFTER 1869

The years following the Fort Laramie Treaty proved to be an uneasy peace. Promises by the government were soon broken. Rations did not materialize. Miners, hunters, and settlers invaded land that had been promised to the Indians. Some of the worst fighting in the West took place during the next two decades. This series of last-ditch bloody battles revolved around U.S. Army attempts to send native people to reservations or to bring back those who had fled.

After years of misunderstanding, open confrontation broke out between Chief Joseph and angry Oregon settlers. In 1877, 200 cavalry pursued Chief Joseph and 800 men, women, and children across the Bitterroot Mountains into Montana. The Indians were in a desperate 1,300-mile race to escape to Canada, where they hoped to seek protection from the government there. In spite of wintry conditions and low food supplies, Chief Joseph managed to evade troops and conduct an amazing guerrilla campaign for four months. On October 5, 1877, he and the other fugitives finally stopped running. "It is cold and we have no blankets. The little children are freezing to death...," Chief Joseph said in his surrender statement. "Hear me, my chiefs. I am tired; my heart is sick and sad. From where the sun now stands I will fight no more forever."

Continued Indian resistance to white invasion of tribal lands all over the West became a mounting source of humiliation and aggravation for the government and the U.S. Army. Indians led by chiefs such as Apache leader Geronimo used superb guerrilla tactics. They appeared without warning, attacked, and disappeared into the deserts and mesas they knew so well. Only the most foolish soldiers dared follow.

After the Civil War, a network of U.S. Army forts had been created. However, leadership in these forts was often muddled. Troops were ill fed, ill housed, and poorly disciplined. Soldiers frequently deserted at the first chance to try their luck in nearby gold and silver mines.

In the meantime, President Ulysses S. Grant had insisted on a new "peace policy" toward Indians when he was elected in 1868. He even created a commission of church leaders to help bring the Indians onto reservations and make them into proper white Christian farmers. This scheme failed miserably.

Beginning in 1869 and during each passing year, more roads, fences, ranches, farms, and towns sprang up in the West. The problem became where to relocate Indians so that they would not come into contact with white settlers. In 1867, Senator L. M. Morrill (1815–1883) of Maine stated the problem bluntly: "We have come to this point in the history of the country that there is no place beyond the population to which you can remove the Indian…and the precise question is, will you exterminate him, or will you fix an abiding place for him?"

The government was uncertain what to do. Goodwill of Indian commissioners constantly backfired. Indian agencies that ran reservations were often controlled by corrupt individuals who skimmed profits from government-issued food and clothing and lined their own pockets. The government estimated that it had spent nearly $1 million for every Indian slain—an expensive, inhumane solution backed by some military professionals, such as General Philip Sheridan (1831–1888), General Sherman's right-hand man, who said in 1869, "The only good Indians I ever saw were dead."

On September 23, 1868, General Sherman wrote a letter to his brother, Senator John Sherman: "The Indian War on the plains need simply amount to this. We have now selected and provided reservations for all, off the roads. All who cling to their old hunting grounds are hostile and will remain till killed off…we must take no chances and clean out Indians as we encounter them."

One recent historian has estimated that in just thirty-eight years, from 1848 to 1886, the Indians in the West lost their fight against whites and had most of their land taken from them. With the coming of the railroad, the invasion of the Western homelands of Indians accelerated and reached a crisis point.

For Indians in the West, these years would be later described as the closing in, a time of yearning for the return of the buffalo, for reunion with relatives who had died, for the experience of living free in open lands now fenced and settled. "Our Indian life," a Hidatsa woman named Buffalo Bird Woman said, "I know, is gone forever."

INDIANS AND THE EXPEDITIONS

Jackson remained fascinated by Indians. He was encouraged to take pictures of tribespeople he encountered throughout his eight years of work with Hayden's expeditions. Sometimes his luck held. Sometimes it did not.

During the 1874 expedition to the Rockies of Colorado, Jackson often discovered that chance encounters with Indians did not provide enough time or the right circumstances to set up cumbersome equipment and sensitize plates. On one occasion, Jackson's skittish pack mules stampeded when they came upon a large group of Utes traveling with travois and ponies.

Even when conditions seemed right for photography, success was often elusive. In late August 1874, in the broad meadowlands of Los Piños Creek, Jackson discovered an encampment of Utes: "70 lodges in all, scattered all over the plain, for at least a square mile." Jackson and his assistants rode into the Los Piños Indian Agency, which was a handful of log buildings plastered with mud. He immediately made friends with the agent, who introduced him to Chief Ouray. The powerful Ute chief lived in a small adobe house in one corner of the square.

Jackson set up a little "gallery" on the agent's porch and took pictures of the agent's family. Then he took a photograph of Chief Ouray and his wife, Chipeta. Ouray had discarded his usual "civilized" clothing of black broadcloth and boots and instead wore his finest beaded buckskin outfit with long fringe

trailing from his arms and shoulders. Chipeta's soft white doeskin dress was decorated with thick white fringe, beadwork, and intricate porcupine-quill embroidery. She seemed nervous and shy in front of the camera, but Jackson was able to take both her picture and her husband's before a storm came up and the picture-taking session ended.

The next day, trouble broke out. When Jackson tried to approach other members of the tribe to get additional photographs, many vehemently refused. Finally, by buying blankets from them, he set up his camera and made a few negatives. A storm suspended his work.

Tensions increased the next day when again Jackson persisted in trying to get some more candid pictures of ponies and children. When he photographed the papoose of a head man named Pe-ah and his wife, the Ute became irate. He dragged his wife and child away. Indian men arrived, "protesting vehemently," Jackson said, "taking hold of the camera and preventing me from either focussing or making an exposure."

In 1870 an encampment of Shoshone set up tepees near South Pass, Wyoming. Jackson also met and photographed the tribal chief Washakie.

The Indians were furious. "Peah kept on exclaiming that the Indians *no sabe* picture, making all Indians *heap sick*," Jackson wrote. The camera was believed to have disastrous powers if used to photograph the village, squaws, or children. Only warriors in small groups could be photographed.

In spite of this warning, Jackson foolishly persisted in trying to take more pictures. He withdrew to a cookhouse and pointed the camera out the entrance. When the Indians noticed what he was doing, they galloped around the building on horseback. They threw a blanket across the doorway.

Finally Jackson gave up. He put away his camera and simply stood about, sheepishly watching the Indians as they lined up to receive their rations.

Communication was a real problem on this trip, perhaps because Jackson had an unskilled interpreter or perhaps because the agent was gone and could not assist him in setting up the photographs the way other photographers had in the past. It was only on the last day of

Chipeta (1843–1924), wife of Ute Chief Ouray, traveled with her husband several times to Washington, D.C., for tribal negotiations. Beautiful and intelligent, she was said to hold a place of honor among whites and Indians alike.

Jackson's visit that he was able to talk at length with anyone in the tribe. A chief, who called himself Billy, visited Jackson and his men after dinner.

Billy was eager to know when the pesky photographer and his assistants would be leaving. He told Jackson that the Utes were angered by "the encroachments of the white men, the miners & the toll roads particularly. [They] found fault with the hunters who came in and took away their game." Clearly, the promises of the 1868 treaty that gave the Utes territory in Colorado west of the 107th meridian were already being broken.

Tensions were building. Like so many other major tribes in the West, the Utes felt frustrated by continued settler invasion and broken treaty promises. Jackson could not have failed to notice that Indian attacks had already scared off many settlers along the trail that he and his men followed as they had approached the Los Piños agency. In his diary Jackson noted numerous abandoned cabins and weed-choked gardens.

Jackson, perhaps unwisely, did not fear for his own safety. A year later, when the expedition returned to the same area, part of Hayden's group would not be so lucky in avoiding the wrath of the Utes. By 1875, tensions had increased considerably. Near the Sierra Abajo, a small group of surveyors had been attacked for thirty-six hours in a standoff. A few mules were killed and equipment was smashed, but the surveyors managed to escape uninjured.

Mistrust and anger against the U.S. government simmered among many different Western tribes. The flash point came in 1876 in the hills of central Montana along the Little Big Horn River. There, a united military encampment of an estimated 15,000 Sioux and Cheyenne warriors wiped out 265 cavalry soldiers. Included among the slain officers was flashy General George A. Custer (1839–1876), the thirty-six-year-old "boy general" who had led the soldiers' ill-planned charge into the Indian camp. Custer was immediately made into a national martyr. Public outrage over "Custer's Last Stand" helped push the government to launch an even more exhaustive effort to wipe out all Indian resistance.

LOST CITIES

In September 1874, Jackson and his assistants were on their way to southern Colorado to photograph a silver-mining region near the La Plata River. At the last minute, Jackson decided to make a detour. A miner had told him where to find Indian ruins and cliff dwellings long rumored to exist near the hidden canyons of Mesa Verde. He could not pass up the opportunity.

The long, rugged journey through Mancos Canyon turned up only a few shards of pottery and the remains of ancient walls. Jackson was disappointed. On September 9, he wrote in his diary: "Had found nothing that really came up to my idea of the grand or picturesque for photos & began to feel a little doubtful & discouraged." At dinner that night, one of the men suddenly pointed up to the canyon wall and cried, "I see it!"

Jackson, too, saw "something that appeared very like a house." Overhead, benches of sandstone rose one atop the other to a height of 800 feet. The house was perched in a crevice "like a swallow's or bat's nest."

The group scrambled up the canyon walls for a better look. "For the first 600 feet or so we had a stiff climb but not a difficult one," Jackson wrote. "Then we found ourselves facing a flat, vertical wall rising some 200 feet above the ledge on which we were standing. Fifty feet above our heads, in a shallow cave, was a two-story house. But how to reach it?"

The 1874 photography division on its way to Mesa Verde and Los Pinos included (left to right) teenage assistants Frank Smart and Ed Anthony, a helper listed as "Mitchell, another called "Whan," writer and naturalist Ernest Ingersoll, Charlie the Cook, and Jackson.

They waited until the light of the next morning to attempt the final ascent. Fearlessly, Jackson and his assistants lugged camera equipment and crawled along a twenty-inch ledge hundreds of feet up the canyon wall. The result was some of Jackson's most spectacular photographs. He was so fascinated by the ruins, he returned in 1875 to take more pictures. Hayden insisted when Jackson returned to Washington, D.C., that he and six assistants spend six months constructing plaster models of the ruins for display at the 1876 Centennial Exhibition in Philadelphia. Especially after the news of the Battle of Little Big Horn, Jackson's popular "educational" displays of cliff dwellings must have seemed romantic and nonthreatening. Exhibition viewers crowded around the "Lost Cities," admiring the relics of Indians who had vanished.

Jackson did not realize until several years later how close he and his assistants had come to uncovering the largest cliff palaces of all. Because they never left the main Mancos Canyon, they missed Mesa Verde. These stunning cliff dwellings were stumbled upon in 1888 by two cattlemen. Jackson would one day have the satisfaction of knowing, however, that his photographs and displays helped foster public support and interest in preserving this mysterious place. In 1906, Congress set aside 52,000 acres containing the cliff dwellings as a national park.

In 1875 neither Jackson nor his contemporaries were certain who originally lived in the ancient cliff dwellings near Mancos Canyon in Montezuma County, Colorado. Scientists now believe that the dwellings may have been inhabited by ancient native people called Anasazi as early as 500 B. C. E.

Jackson returned again to the southwest in 1877 to photograph the Hopi pueblos near Santa Fe, New Mexico. To save on weight and cumbersome developing, he decided to use the new dry-tissue process of developing on this trip. He carried an eight-by-ten-inch camera and was able to pack all his supplies on his back. In spite of the care he took in handling the new film, when he returned to Washington, D.C., he discovered that every single one of the 400 images he had taken was blank. "It still makes me feel sick, in a very real, physical sense," Jackson said, remembering the moment when he knew that the entire summer had been a complete failure. "My experience of 1877 was quite the most costly setback of my career."

In spite of this major disappointment, in 1877 he published the exhaustive 124-page *Descriptive Catalogue of Photographs of North American Indians*. This book contained lists of his own collections of negatives as well as photographs of Indians he had purchased from other photographers.

(left) *The Cliff Palace, Mesa Verde, Colorado, was not set aside as part of a 50,000-acre national park until 1906.*

(right) *Jackson or his assistant reached the Temple of Isis at the top of a steep canyon wall, and recorded Manitou Canyon, outside of Colorado Springs, Colorado. The photo is undated.*

013835. THE ELKTON MINE, CRIPPLE CREEK, COLO.

CHAPTER NINE

BOOM AND BUST: MINING TOWNS AND WESTERN CITIES

*The mountain side was so steep that [Virginia City, Nevada] had a
slant to it like a roof. Each street was a terrace, and from each to the next
street below the descent was forty or fifty feet....It was a laborious climb,
in that thin atmosphere, to ascend from D to A Street, and you were
panting and out of breath when you got there; but you could turn
around and go down again like a house a-fire...*
—Mark Twain
   Roughing It, 1861

In 1878, thirty-five-year-old Jackson reached a crossroads in his career. Hayden and the survey had run out of funding. There would not be another expedition. On November 23, 1878, Jackson's second child, Louise, was born in Washington, D.C. His son, Clarence, had just turned two. Jackson needed to find a new job.

How much Jackson's wife contributed to his sudden zeal for higher pay can only be guessed. His top salary with the expedition had been just $125 per month. Jackson admitted in his autobiography, "Emilie, always loyal and comprehending, surely deserved something better of marriage than a husband who was away five, six, seven months every year."

Jackson decided to open a commercial studio in Denver, a city he'd first seen in 1870, when five thou-

(facing page) Elkton Mine outside of Cripple Creek, Colorado, eventually yielded more than $13 million in gold. After 1895, barren hills dotted with gray mine dumps surrounded the area.

sand gold seekers huddled in cottonwood log cabins along Cherry Creek. Another visitor around the same time was not as impressed when she laid eyes on the "Queen of the Plains," as Denverites liked to call their city. "I looked down where the great braggart city lay spread out, brown and treeless upon brown and treeless plain which seemed to nourish nothing but wormwood and Spanish bayonet," wrote forty-one-year-old English traveler and writer Isabella Bird (1832–1904), who eventually climbed Longs Peak, the highest peak in the Rockies.

When Bird entered Denver's downtown, her opinion improved. She was pleased to find out that shoot-outs had become rare and no one had been lynched from the lampposts in several years. Even so, Denver still had the flavor of a frontier town. She noted that there was a band of Utes encamped on the outskirts. More than fifty stores made up the downtown. Hotels and boardinghouses were filled with invalids who came to the high, dry mountain air to take the "camp cure." The crowds in the streets were "almost solely masculine," noted Bird, who saw only five white women all day.

Bird, like Jackson, encountered many different kinds of people in Denver. There were "hunters and trappers in buckskin clothing; men of the Plains with belts and revolvers, in great blue cloaks, relics of the [Civil] war; teamsters in leathern suits; horsemen in fur coats and cuts and buffalo-hide boots with the hair outside and camping blankets behind their huge Mexican saddles; Broadway dandies in light kid gloves; rich English sporting tourists, clean, comely and supercilious looking..."

By 1876, three different railroad lines connected Denver to points west, east, and south. Denver's population skyrocketed to 35,000. The city's bustling, ambitious spirit was best characterized by a store owner's sign hanging in the window that said: "Gone to bury my wife. Back in half an hour."

Jackson launched his studio business in 1879. By then, Denver proudly boasted of plank sidewalks, telephones, and the regular services of a water-sprinkle cart to keep down ever present dust on the unpaved streets. People continued to pour into Denver. By 1890 the population would more than double: 106,700.

Jackson's studio thrived. He was paid to photograph the splendid new buildings going up in Denver's downtown and residential areas for booster brochures and booklets. He bought and obtained rights to negatives from numerous other photographers so that his studio owned the most complete collection of images of every scenic wonder in the West. By 1886, he was described by the *Rocky Mountain News* as "Denver's renowned landscape photographer." The studio expanded repeatedly during its first fifteen years as Jackson published more and more of his Western views in books, magazines, and souvenir brochures.

He bought Emilie a suitably fancy black satin-and-velvet outfit to wear to parties and built her a big brick house in a fashionable Denver neighborhood, complete with two parlors decorated with the latest bric-a-brac—from china dogs to peacock feathers. He hired plenty of servants. He even sent his three children, including the last, a daughter named Hallie who was born in 1882, to boarding school.

Even with so much financial success, Jackson felt restless. And no wonder. Every time he looked out the window of his studio, he saw the Rockies in the distance. Undoubtedly Jackson would have agreed with Isabella Bird, who noted the "glorious view" of the mountains from the city, then added, "I should hate even to spend a week [in Denver]. The sight of those glories so near and yet out of reach would make me nearly crazy."

With the increasing demands of a successful business, Jackson had less time to work "in some great open country" the way he liked. Thanks in part to the effectiveness of his stunning photographs, more and more people were coming West to live or visit. As a result, capturing the uncluttered, uncivilized West with his camera became more difficult.

To satisfy his wanderlust, he took railroad publicity jobs that allowed him to travel far from the confines of his studio. But instead of sleeping under bridges the way he had while traveling with Arundel Hull in 1869, Jackson now had his own fancy, private railroad car complete with a darkroom, a servant, and enough space to take his whole family. Once he even brought along his seventy-year-old mother.

"She stuck to the observation platform, cinders and all," he later wrote, "as zestfully as her grandchildren."

SMALL-TOWN OPTIMISM

Throughout his career, Jackson witnessed primitive Western settlements transform overnight into industrial complexes when gold or silver was discovered. Sometimes all it took was the arrival of the railroad. Whether or not these little Western towns eventually grew into thriving cities or withered overnight into ghost towns did not seem to worry early town planners and boosters. The optimism of the Gilded Age was powerful in the West.

Jackson (far right) in 1883 traveled in considerable luxury with friends and family in a private railroad car that was part of a photography expedition to Mexico.

"In every bar-room," Rudyard Kipling noticed on his journey west in 1889, "lay a copy of the local paper, and every copy impressed upon the inhabitants...that they were the best, finest, bravest, richest, and most progressive town of the most progressive nation under Heaven." Kipling became so tired of every Western town claiming to be "Queen City of the Prairie," he complained, "I wish Americans didn't tell such useless lies."

Jackson's earliest small-town photographs were a series of stereo views he made of Corinne, Utah, in 1869. The street view reveals hastily built storefronts, tent roofs, and hopeful oversized signs for a watchmaker, jeweler, tin shop, and painter. There was even a giant wooden gun to represent a gunsmith's services.

A few years later, a train passenger stood on the platform and looked out at the same town in the moonlight and wrote: "There is not much to see: the long, low station buildings; the shabby shops; the staring, square, white saloons from whose windows blaze the brightest lights in the whole town."

Small Western towns like Corinne often began as nothing more than "a dozen log houses arranged in no order," according to Jackson. A railroad engineer named William Walk, who worked on the Denver and Rio Grande, wrote in 1873, "Some of the early towns I went to were nothing but mud holes. I watched Creede [a town in the San Juan Mountains] grow from a patch of willows to a city of thousands in six months."

Jackson discovered that fire was often one of the most devastating events in the lives of mountain settlements. There was little available water and no one took the time to stop prospecting to organize fire departments. In 1874, Jackson passed through Central City, Colorado, once called "the richest square mile on Earth." He recorded that the thriving gold mining town "had completely burned to the ground." The citizens of Central City later rebuilt many of the town's buildings with fireproof brick.

Wind-blown, dusty Corinne, Utah, was recorded in 1869 in this stereographic view.

LEADVILLE, COLORADO: LIFE CYCLE OF A MINING TOWN

Jackson first visited Leadville, Colorado, in 1873 as part of the Hayden expeditions. He returned in 1879. The contrast in his impressions is remarkable and reveals something about the stark contrasts in the boom-and-bust cycle of so many mining towns.

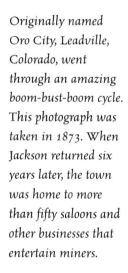

Originally named Oro City, Leadville, Colorado, went through an amazing boom-bust-boom cycle. This photograph was taken in 1873. When Jackson returned six years later, the town was home to more than fifty saloons and other businesses that entertain miners.

Located 10,000 feet above sea level on the headwaters of the Arkansas River, this "wild pine flat" was the place where Leadville had its start. Originally named Oro City for an early gold strike, the settlement had thinned to only 200 hardy souls by the time Jackson arrived in 1873. The place was so deserted, he had trouble finding anyone willing to sell him and his hungry assistants anything to eat.

In 1874 when silver was discovered in the thick sand that clogged the sluice boxes used for finding gold, Leadville's luck suddenly changed. By the time Jackson returned in 1879, the town was booming. Leadville was in the peak of its glory. In 1879 alone, more than $11 million in silver was removed from the thirty local working mines. There were 14,800 people living in town—10,600 of whom were men under age thirty. By 1880, an estimated 40,000 people were living and working in Leadville.

Jackson must have been flabbergasted to see that the once sleepy, deserted town now had twenty-eight miles of streets, gaslights, five churches, and three hospitals. Day and night, the air rang with the sound of hammers and axes and the earsplitting, steam-powered mining drills known as widow-makers. Sawmills buzzed, creating yard after yard of yellow pine boards used to build everything from slipshod shacks to sidewalks. Meanwhile, seventeen belching smelters consumed tons of coal and filled the sky with stinking clouds of gas and soot.

Outside town stood a wilderness of miners' tents and wigwams of boughs and bare poles. There were cabins wedged between stumps and cabins built on stumps. There were cabins half roofed and cabins with sailcloth roofs and cabins with no roofs at all.

Scattered in the mountains were two thousand lumberjacks who quickly cut down every available tree to use for fuel or construction purposes. Meadows were being transformed into hay ranches to feed the thousands of work animals needed. Livestock and vegetable growers farmed every possible acre, yet the population was still dependent on food shipped over the steep pass. Rivers were diverted into canals for irrigation or mining operations, which created turbid yellow streams.

"Scattered over the hill at the foot of Mosquito Pass," Jackson wrote, "were miners' shacks, derricks, ore dumps and a few stunted pine trees. I photographed them all."

In many respects the life of a miner in Leadville was not so different from that of the factory worker in the East. These "fortune-seekers," as Jackson called them, spent ten-hour days deep in Leadville's mines, where the work was hard, dirty, and dangerous. The first miners in Leadville were mostly German-, Irish-, Cornish- and Canadian-born. Later, Serbs and Croats from Eastern Europe, and later

still, Mexicans, would come to the mines to work. Chinese were not allowed. The Leadville miners soon discovered that expensive shoe leather rotted quickly in the wet, dripping mines. Many dressed in rubber coats and hats to keep dry. For their trouble, they were paid as little as two dollars a day by the large corporations that ran the mines and operated company stores, where miners could buy high-priced food on credit.

Mining families lived in rows of drab, identical houses "jammed side by side behind weedy yards ironically overlooking magnificent panoramas," one historian wrote. Their worst dread was contagious diseases like diphtheria, which would sweep through mining towns like wildfire. Accidental blasts, cave-ins, and fires in heavily timbered underground mines—not to mention the possibility of catching pneumonia from breathing flying silica from the drills—made life in Leadville's mines precarious at best.

In 1880, one year after Jackson took his photographs of Leadville, the miners' union organized their first strike. They demanded an eight-hour day and uniform pay of four dollars a day. The miners walked off their jobs and closed down the mine. They said they would not return until their demands were met. Two weeks later the governor of Colorado called in the state militia, put Leadville under military law, and brutally ended the strike by jailing 160 miners.

In the less than a decade, Leadville's silver was exhausted. People moved out. In the late 1890s there were a few small scattered gold strikes, but the rollicking boom days seemed to be gone for good. By the turn of the century, it was possible to buy a building in Leadville for a just a few dollars. Nobody was interested in real estate, however. The houses were chopped up for kindling.

(facing page) Hydraulic mining near Virginia City, Montana, in 1871 blasted away the sides of Alder Gulch with water. Heavy soil erosion polluted many nearby streams and rivers.

In 1892 Jackson took this photograph of two explorers gazing out over the sunlit Grand Canyon of the Colorado.

CHAPTER TEN
"EVERYWHERE I GO":
THE CHANGING FACE OF THE FRONTIER

*Everywhere I go in the Yellowstone country, twice on long drives to the
south and east, within the past few weeks, tells me this, that soon if I am
to gallop the little gray mare it must be in a lane, and you do not care,
but I do; that makes me sad. I would there were yet a few waste places
left untouched by the settler and his cursed wire fence, good in its way,
but not for me. I can not help it.*
—L. A. Huffman (1854–1931)
The Yellowstone Journal, July 8, 1907

The trip that William Henry Jackson and landscape painter Thomas Moran planned for the summer of 1892 was something of a hopeful, boyish dream.

The two old friends—Jackson, nearly fifty, and Moran, almost fifty-five but with a long, flowing white beard that made him appear much older—were returning together to Yellowstone, the place that had helped make them both famous. On the way, they would stop at the Grand Canyon in Arizona. Jackson hoped to take as many photos as possible. Moran's goal was to sketch continuously. He would take his drawings and inspiration back to his New Jersey studio to create enormous, wall-sized oil paintings.

To make the trip economically feasible, Jackson and Moran had cobbled together sponsorship from the Santa Fe Railroad and the state of Wyoming, both of which were interested in "scenic wonders" for their exhibits at the 1893 World's Columbian Exposition to be held in Chicago.

What neither Jackson nor Moran had taken into account was that they were both twenty years older than they were on their trip with the Hayden expedition in 1871. They had changed. The West had changed, too.

At first, their journey seemed to contain all the promise and triumph of those heady early years. On May 27, Jackson, Moran, Moran's twenty-eight-year-old son Paul and Jackson's young assistant descended five thousand feet from the rim of the Grand Canyon to the Colorado River. They hiked a path that zigzagged and plummeted between six waterfalls. "We let ourselves down with ropes," Moran wrote to his wife. "Jackson's photos will show you how we did it. We reached the river about four in the afternoon. It was very full and muddy and it seemed to me that the rapids were equal to the whirlpool rapids at

Niagara. Black lava 2000 feet in height was all around us except an occasional glimpse of the higher sandstone peaks in the openings...a glorious trip."

To celebrate, Moran quickly created *In the Lava Beds*, a remarkably revealing watercolor only ten-by-thirteen inches in size. In the painting, hostile cliffs tower over grazing packhorses. A small group of travelers lingers together as if joking and talking. Smoke rises from their campfire. Jackson's camera, like a lonely solitary eye, stands on three spindly legs in the foreground and observes the

Bright Angel Trail in Grand Canyon, Arizona, was a popular excursion for the bravest tourists. By 1900 there would be rail service to the edge of the canyon.

scene—not so different from the unmanned robotic probe that would one day rove Mars.

After spending a week in the Grand Canyon, Jackson and Moran impatiently made their way toward Yellowstone. Their group had grown to include a cook, a packer, and three commissioners from the Wyoming Columbian Exposition. The unwieldy crowd traveled in high style in a private railroad car and later in a stagecoach. There were drawbacks to the luxury, however. Jackson and Moran soon found that they were slaves to the train's schedule and route. They did not have enough time to explore and linger where they wished.

At their first opportunity, Jackson and Moran made their escape. While waiting in Gillette, Wyoming, for the next available transportation to take them to Yellowstone, they decided to enjoy a side trip to Devils Tower—fifty miles away. The only person they took along was Jackson's young assistant. Jackson and Moran rented a pair of broken-down horses and packed a light wagon with cameras and art supplies. They brought no food.

This would be their first mistake.

Their second mistake was in not asking for better directions. By then there was no longer just one main road through the hills and buttes of this part of Wyoming. There were many. "A map is a sorry guide to follow in a country devoted to cattle-raising," Moran later wrote, "where roads branch out everywhere and seem to end nowhere." After twenty-eight miles behind a "startling indifferent" team, Jackson and Moran realized they'd gone too far to turn back. And Devils Tower was still nowhere in sight.

In the old days, Jackson had always been able to buy whatever supplies he had needed to feed himself, his assistants, and his horses from friendly ranchers along the way. But things had changed. Empty cottonwood cabins and leaning fenceposts were all that remained of the ranching boom that had ended after too many deadly droughts and blizzards. From 1886 to 1888, months of below-zero winter temperatures, high winds, and deep snow froze, starved, or suffocated millions of head of cattle from Colorado to the Canada border, from the 100th meridian to the Pacific Slope.

Cowmen went flat broke. Many never recovered. Some, like Granville Stuart of Montana, walked away from their homesteads, vowing, "I never wanted to own again an animal I couldn't feed and shelter." A few stockmen with sizable landholdings stayed. Meanwhile, cowboys who'd lost their jobs with cattle outfits tried homesteading smaller sections to see if they could make it on their own.

By the time Jackson and Moran arrived in Wyoming in 1892, an undeclared war was simmering between the small landowners or "nesters" and the big cattle outfits. Nesters claimed the cattle kings were illegally using the best grasslands and trying to intimidate them with hired gunmen. The big stockmen claimed the homesteaders were stealing their cattle and branding them as their own.

Unfortunately, neither Jackson nor Moran seemed aware of this situation as they wandered the Wyoming countryside in search of Ranch 101, a place they'd been told might provide them with something to eat. With empty stomachs, they pushed over the next ridge, hoping for any sign of human habitation. Finally they found a neatly painted frame building surrounded by well-kept outbuildings and barns. But when they knocked at the door, they soon discovered another new reality about the West.

Instead of being greeted with customary Western hospitality, Jackson and Moran were confronted by the ranch's hostile superintendent, who refused to even give them directions or sell them food. "His reply was rather chilling," Moran reported. "He said that he did not run a road-house."

This ranch was part of a network of thousands of acres owned by a growing group of distant Eastern corporations that bought land from smaller ranchers who had gone bankrupt or were intimidated into leaving. The aridity of the West meant that it took eighty-eight acres to provide enough grass to feed just one cow. A landowner needed thousands of acres to survive in the cattle business—even in a good year when beef prices were high and the cattle managed to survive the brutal winters.

As the sun began to set, Jackson and Moran bumped and rolled along, hungry and exhausted. They followed Cabin Creek, a dried-up stream dotted with dozens of deserted ranches. After taking a fork in the road, they caught a glimpse of Devils Tower about twenty-five miles away—and something more ominous: a dark mass of clouds rising in the west. In moments they were surrounded by lightning and thunder and pelted by hail. "Light summer clothing and thin felt hats were our only protection against this awful fuselage of ice-balls," Moran wrote.

By the time the skies cleared, the ground had turned into Wyoming gumbo—"the blackest, stickiest, most India-rubber-like mud that exists on earth." After stopping many times to chop and scrape gumbo that clogged the wagon wheels, they made their way to a small group of pines on a hill. They built a fire, dried themselves off, and spent the night without any supper.

It took them until early afternoon the next day before they spotted smoke rising from a chimney of a house. "We had had no food for thirty-eight hours," Moran complained. Luckily, the ranch owner was happy to feed them and informed them that they had been traveling on the wrong side of the river. After a long hard drive

After a harrowing journey in 1892, Jackson and Moran finally found Devils Tower in northern Wyoming.

that afternoon, they found lodging with another hospitable rancher, an elegant Englishman who raised horses and owned a grand piano.

They finally located Devils Tower, a fluted gray column of stone that looked like a petrified stump rising 2,000 feet above the Belle Fourche River. Known as *Mato Tipi* or Bear Lodge by the Lakota, this land-

Yellowstone's first large hotel, photographed in 1892, was completed near the Mammoth Hot Springs in 1884, and would eventually boast having the first electric lights.

mark was the setting for an ancient Kiowa legend. The legend told how seven young sisters playing near the spot were suddenly chased by bears. The little girls jumped on the rock to escape, praying that it would grow tall and save them. The rock cooperated and rose higher and higher as the frustrated bears clawed its sides, creating deep grooves. Eventually the rock grew so tall that the girls became a constel-

1. MAMMOTH HOT SPRINGS LOWER BASINS. LOOKING UP.

This photo of Mammoth Hot Springs Lower Basin in Yellowstone was taken in 1878. In 1892 it was difficult to set up shots of the hot springs without encountering souvenir stands.

lation of stars called the Seven Sisters by the Kiowa, but known as the Pleiades, in the constellation Taurus, to people of European ancestry.

Jackson and Moran found the legendary gray rock fascinating. "We sketched and photographed it during the remainder of the day," Moran said. The next morning, they returned from "their adventurous journey" to Gillette—weary but wiser.

At last, on July 20, after more than two weeks in the saddle, they reached Yellowstone. In his first letter to his wife upon his arrival, Moran wrote, "I have not yet gone up to look at the Springs, but from the Hotel it looks as if they had lost the color they had originally."

Color was not the only thing that had changed in Yellowstone. The place crawled with tourists who rode bumper to bumper in tour wagons along regular routes from springs to canyon, from falls and lakes to geysers. Of course, it was possible to avoid the crowds by hiking into the wilderness away from the popular sights. Anyone who did so risked ridicule, however, from the finely dressed ladies who hung about the luxurious Yellowstone hotels. A few years earlier, President Chester A. Arthur (1829–1886) had caused quite a scene when he returned shabby and dirty after roughing it in Yellowstone's back country. Jackson and Moran had given up on roughing it by the time they arrived. "I stayed at the Hotel in preference to camp, as did Jackson and a couple of the others," Moran wrote to his wife on July 26. "We have all had enough of camp life."

The two artists soon found they were celebrities as they tried to photograph and sketch Yellowstone. "I have been made much of at all the places in the park as the great and only 'Moran' *the* painter of the Yellowstone and I am looked at curiously by all the people at the Hotels," Moran bragged to his wife.

Jackson must have felt frustrated as he struggled to focus his mammoth eighteen-by-twenty-two-inch camera while gawking tourists milled about the scene. How could he ever recapture the untouched Yellowstone of twenty years before with so many people in the way? As he worked, he soon discovered another startling change. He was being photographed. Tourists crowded about him with their own little cameras, the new, easy-to-use Kodak ("You Press the Button, We Do the Rest") that cost twenty-five dollars. This faddish device, invented in 1888 by George Eastman, allowed anyone to take their own vacation pictures and have them developed by the manufacturer for only ten dollars.

IRON-HEARTED POWER: THE TERROR OF STEEL AND STEAM

Jackson was keenly aware of other changes that had occurred in the West as well. Railroad construction had tripled in the U.S. since 1870. With heavy government sponsorship, more than 160,000 miles of track connected cities by 1890. However, Americans' love affair with the train was over.

The railroad colonization of the West had created more than two million farms by the 1880s. But by the end of that decade, the price paid for farm products suffered a sharp decline. Corn that originally sold for one dollar a bushel in the early 1870s sold for only ten cents a bushel ten years later. Settlers felt helpless and angry. It wasn't long before Westerners, who had originally regarded the Great Iron Horse with gratitude, now understood what a stranglehold the railroad had on their lives.

Everything Western farmers produced had to be transported by rail. Train monopolies set shipping prices. As a result, by the 1880s it cost farmers more to ship grain from Dakota Territory to Chicago than it did to ship grain from Chicago to Liverpool, England. Railroad companies also indirectly controlled how much grain dealers would pay farmers for their yields. The railroad controlled freight charges that small local businesses had to pay to receive merchandise they needed for their stores. Railroad monopolies backed and helped elect government officials and bribed newspapers.

Westerners had become outraged by the findings of Congress, which investigated the Credit

Mobilier in the 1870s. This group of speculators, once known as "visionary businessmen," had organized construction of the transcontinental railroad. They made themselves into millionaires with phony construction and supply contracts—netting a profit of nearly 300 percent—all at American taxpayers' expense.

Anti-railroad sentiment helped spur countless strikes and work stoppages or walkouts. After a wage cut in July 1877, the first railroad worker strike was launched on a national scale. This strike roared like a firestorm across the country from Baltimore to San Francisco. The railroad ran again only after federal troops were called in. Hundreds of strikers were killed; thousands of workers were blacklisted. Millions of dollars in property were destroyed. Between 1881 and 1905, 37,000 strikes involving an estimated seven million workers took place all over America.

By 1892, farmers in the Midwest and West had organized the Populist Party to elect their own presidential candidate, James B. Weaver of Iowa. Although unsuccessful, the attempt allowed Westerners to flex their political muscles for the first time.

While the railroad in the West could be seen as a symbol of progress, it was also a symbol of poverty and powerlessness—a haunting contrast. California journalist Frank Norris (1870–1902) best described the changing Western opinion about the railroad in his best-selling book *The Octopus* (1901). The railroad had become a

galloping monster, the terror of steel and steam, with its singular eye—Cyclopean, red, shooting from horizon to horizon...the symbol of a vast power, huge, terrible, flinging the echo of its thunder over the reaches of the valley, leaving blood and destruction in its path, the leviathan, with tentacles of steel clutching into the soil, the iron-hearted Power, the monster, the Colossus, the Octopus.

40.

CHAPTER ELEVEN

1893: THE WHITE CITY AND THE END OF THE FRONTIER

*And now, four centuries from the discovery of America, at the end of a
hundred years of life under the Constitution, the frontier has gone, and
with its going has closed the first period of American history.*
—Frederick Jackson Turner (1861–1932)
"The Significance of the Frontier in American History," 1893

In 1893, when silver mines closed in Colorado because of decreased demands overseas, more than 30,000 people roamed the streets in cities and small towns in that state, looking for work. Nobody had money for photographs. William Henry Jackson discovered that his newly expanded studio in Denver was about to go belly-up.

As a nearly bankrupt businessman, Jackson was not alone. That year more than 15,000 big and small businesses nationwide collapsed during the worst depression the country had ever experienced. By the end of the year, more than 600 banks had closed their doors as the value of the silver dollar plummeted to only sixty cents. The stock market panicked and more than seventy-four railroads shut down.

The lifeline for Jackson's business appeared in a most unexpected form: the 1893 World's Columbian Exposition. In spite of a faltering economy, the fair's Chicago organizers went ahead with the enormous six-month extravaganza, celebrating 400 years of America's progress since Columbus landed in the New World in 1492. The White City, as it was called, contained 400 specially constructed white buildings bril-

*(facing page)
In this image of
the Transportation
Building, which
was designed by Louis
Sullivan (1856–1924),
Jackson tried to capture
the scale a Columbian
Exposition visitor
might experience.*

liantly lit with 7,000 arc and 120,000 incandescent lamps. More than 700 acres of swamp along Lake Michigan had been dredged to create gardens, fountains, plazas, promenades, and lagoons with gondolas.

What made the White City even more remarkable was that it had been built just twenty years after the Great Chicago Fire had leveled the downtown, destroying almost $200 million in property and killing 250 people. Chicago, like the mythic bird called the phoenix, seemed to have risen from its own ashes—bigger and better than ever.

At the center of the dazzling white Court of Honor, tourists enjoyed gondola rides in the Great Basin, an enormous man-made pond.

What the fair organizers decided they needed were additional photographs to record the beauty of what had been created. Daniel Burnham (1846–1912), Chicago's leading architect and the fair's director, asked Jackson to take 100 photographs of the buildings and grounds for $1,000. Jackson must have been delighted.

His ten days of shooting in Chicago also gave him a chance to see the display of 100 of his own photos, exhibited as part of the massive railroad celebration in the fair's Transportation Building. In the same building, beside the puny forty-year-old stove boiler engine, stood the latest magnificent 130-ton locomotive capable of speeds of 100 miles per hour—all meant to impress the public with America's railroad progress.

But the fair's total crowd of more than 27 million men, women, and children did not really want educational displays of railroad engines or glimpses of such historic sacred relics as locks of Thomas Jefferson's red hair. They wanted entertainment. And they got it.

On a one-mile strip of land called the Midway, Jackson and others saw sights ranging from genuine Japanese pagodas and South Sea thatch huts to sword swallowers and Bedouin acrobats. There were exhibits of Stone Age people and tableaus of "typical Indian families"—life-size statues of adults and children "working in their own environments." Visitors sipped Dr. Welch's Grape Juice, rode the amazing automatic moving sidewalk, gazed into the biggest telescope in the world, and glided in dizzy circles on the newly invented 250-foot-diameter Ferris wheel. Countless thousands attended one of the most popular events, Little Egypt's scandalous "hoochee-coochee dance," performed in shocking silk trousers.

"I went to the fair at once," one fair-goer wrote in his diary, "and before I had walked two minutes, a bewilderment at the gloriousness of everything seized me...until my mind was dazzled to a standstill."

Buffalo Bill's Wild West Show in Chicago made more money than the most lucrative Columbian Exposition amusements.

BUFFALO BILL'S WILD WEST

If Jackson left the fairgrounds and walked across Sixty-third Street, he could have visited the most dazzling event of all: Buffalo Bill's Wild West Show and Congress of Rough Riders of the World. Considered "too undignified," Buffalo Bill's show was barred by the fair's organizers. No matter. Buffalo Bill crossed the street and rented fourteen acres, built his own grandstand for 18,000 fans and began selling tickets.

"Every day thousands were turned away for lack of seats, and many a visitor paid his way into the Wild West Show, believing it to be the World's Fair," wrote Sir Henry

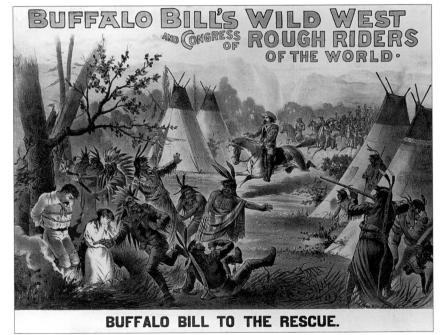

BUFFALO BILL TO THE RESCUE.

Annie Oakley's domestic pose in 1893 outside her "home" during a Wild West Show tour doesn't give an accurate picture of the remarkable woman who shot through dimes tossed in the air as part of her act.

Irving, an enthusiastic Englishman. "Such dare-devil riding was never seen on earth. When the American cowboys sweep like a tornado up the track, forty or fifty strong, every man swinging his hat and every pony at its utmost speed, a roar of wonder and delight breaks from the thousands in the grand stand."

Buffalo Bill, formerly known as William F. Cody, was born in Iowa and raised in Kansas. The year of the fair he was forty-seven years old, a superb shot and excellent horseman, and was described in his advertising as an "exemplar of the strong and unique traits of the true frontiersman."

Audiences loved to watch brave white horsemen turning back attacking hordes of genuine war-painted Arapahos, Cheyennes, and Lakota. "Indians," one historian said, "imitating imitations of themselves." The show included such exciting scenes as "Capture of the Deadwood Mail Coach by the Indians" and "An Attack of the Settler's Cabin." Always popular was the grand finale, "Battle of the Little Big Horn, Showing with Accuracy the Scene of Custer's Last Charge." More than one hundred horsemen from around the globe plus one hundred Indians took part in the rain-or-shine extravaganza that had toured every capital in Europe. But how many Americans in the audience in 1893 noticed that the most famous Indian in Buffalo Bill's troupe was missing?

Sitting Bull (1831–1890), the famous Lakota chief who had led his braves to victory at the Battle of Little Big Horn, was Buffalo Bill's major attraction from 1883 until 1885, when the Standing Rock agent in Dakota Territory ordered Sitting Bull to return to the reservation. Sitting Bull, the agent feared, was becoming too imperial and difficult to manage.

Five years later, in 1890, Sitting Bull was living quietly on the Standing Rock Indian Reservation when the Ghost Dance movement became popular. This new religion promised a revival of the old days—the return of the buffalo and the sudden disappearance of all whites. It was based on a vision of paradise, a land free of sickness and want inhabited by all generations of Indians that had passed away.

After centuries of disease, military defeat, and dislocation, the Indian population had dropped to 237,000, the lowest point since the arrival of the first Europeans. By 1890, reservations were actually shrinking in size. In spite of these facts, Indian agents across the Plains became increasingly worried as more and more Indians took part in frenzied ritualized dancing and chanting. Indians danced in a circle wearing special sacred shirts they believed would stop all bullets. Sitting Bull approved of the dancing and tried to promote it. His involvement made the reservation officials even more nervous. On December 15, 1890, Sitting Bull was killed when Lakota police tried to arrest him.

Sitting Bull's followers and Indians on the nearby Pine Ridge Reservation feared attack from the 5,000 soldiers who were massing nearby. A group of 120 men and 230 women and children camped on Wounded Knee Creek began to perform the Ghost Dance. Soldiers opened fire. The Indians fought back and 25 soldiers were killed. More than 250 Lakota men, women, and children died and were buried in a mass grave. "It was a thing to melt the heart of a man, if it was stone," one soldier remembered, "to see those little children with their bodies shot to pieces."

Unlike what really happened in 1890 at Wounded Knee, Buffalo Bill's Wild West Show portrayed the Indians as aggressive killers. According to the show, whites were always badly abused conquerors who simply retaliated against barbaric massacres.

Buffalo Bill was a storyteller who used characters, symbols, and events about the West that his audiences understood. In his performances, the West was won violently, wrested away from Indians who occupied the land. The tools used to fulfill the American ideal of progress were rifles and bullets. Thanks to hardy pioneers and cowboys, the West was conquered. The frontier days, according to Buffalo Bill, had ended and were gone forever.

WINNING THE WILD WEST: ANOTHER STORY

While Buffalo Bill was performing his show, someone else was telling another version of the Wild West story. His name was Frederick Jackson Turner (1861–1932). He was a slope-shouldered, thirty-two-year-old history instructor from the University of Wisconsin who was taking part in the Columbian Exposition's official educational activities.

William Henry Jackson probably did not attend Turner's speech, which was given as part of the meeting of the American Historical Association and the World's Congress of Historians. The event wasn't very popular. Mostly professors and university presidents attended Turner's talk, which had been dully titled "The Significance of the Frontier in American History." But what Turner said about the West made his listeners go home and rewrite their textbooks.

"The frontier has gone," Turner announced, "and with its going has closed the first period of American history." According to the report written by the Superintendent of the 1890 Census, the frontier had ceased to exist because there was "scarcely any substantial unsettled areas in the U.S."

The nation's evolution, Turner claimed, had depended on the continuous flow of Western colonization made possible by the abundance of free land. "The demand for land and the love of wilderness freedom drew the frontier ever onward." America wasn't just an extension of European civilization. Its frontier defined it and made it different—vibrant and alive. Turner saw the process as a peaceful occupation of a mostly empty continent using tools like the ax and the plow. Unlike Buffalo Bill's version, Indians weren't obstacles. Hostile nature was the main problem.

Both Buffalo Bill and Turner created a simple but dramatic narrative that their audiences could understand. Turner used flowery language and exhorted his listeners to stand at Cumberland Gap and watch

Daniel Boone and his followers make their brave way across the frontier. Buffalo Bill staged wild, fiery scenes to show how pioneers were saved at the last minute from being burned at the stake by "crazed savages." In Turner's version, the contributions of women and minorities were scarcely mentioned. In Buffalo Bill's narrative, minorities like the Mexican cowboy, or vaquero, were given bit parts, never heroic starring roles. Sharpshooter Annie Oakley (1860–1926) might shoot lit cigars from people's mouths, but she never participated in dramatic reenactments. Women in Buffalo Bill's show were rescued, *not* rescuers.

America's progress, Turner and Buffalo Bill said, moved from the primitive to the civilized. The frontier was gone, they claimed. The Wild West had been won.

Of course, there was a disturbing side to both their stories. If there was no more frontier, there could be no return to the primitive, to the natural. Without wilderness, what would happen to the unique, rugged American character? What would keep it vibrant and alive? What happened when the last "real" cowboy, the last "real" Indian, and the last buffalo vanished? What then?

These were uncomfortable questions.

And in 1893, William Henry Jackson's photographs may have held some of the answers.

These "Fine Wild Views"

Like Turner and Buffalo Bill, Jackson was also a masterful storyteller. Anyone who walked over to the Wyoming state exhibit could see that.

More than a dozen photographs taken during Jackson and Moran's trip the summer before were displayed on the walls. These superb pictures showed how much Jackson had matured as an artist. The years on the survey and, later, his own commercial work had clearly boosted his confidence with the mammoth format camera.

(above) William Henry Jackson as he appeared in 1895.

(right) Photographs like this 1892 mammoth double plate panorama taken of Lake de Amelia in Wyoming "entice viewers by their silence, the mysterious beckoning of another world," wrote historian Alan Trachtenberg.

"Jackson's photos were large and better printed than mine, showing his superior facilities," confided Utah photographer Charles Roscoe Savage in his diary entry for September 20, 1893, after viewing Jackson's work. These were "pictures in every sense of the word, and pictures that are once seen and not forgotten," wrote John Nicol in the 1893 issue of *Photo Beacon*.

But it was not just the superior technical quality that captured people's imaginations. Jackson's Western photographs told a story—and not the same story that Turner and Buffalo Bill told. In Jackson's work there was no end to the frontier. There were no conquests, no heroes, no dramatic poses, no flowery phrases or nationalistic jingoes—just the Western landscape itself—mute, silent, beautiful.

Imagine ourselves for a moment at the World's Columbian Exposition. Like Denver visitor Horace G. Benson, we

have been bombarded all day by dizzying sights and deafening noises. "Everything is buzz and clatter and confusion," wrote Benson. "I am dazzled, captivated and bewildered."

Then we step inside the Wyoming state exhibit and view Jackson's mammoth, two-plate, seventeen-by-forty-inch photograph, *Lake de Amelia*. Something happens. Something different. It's as if a curtain has been thrown open, revealing a new view through the window.

Standing in front of this photograph is like falling into space. The longer we immerse ourselves in the huge image, the more we feel inserted into the landscape of limpid lake and distant mountains. Nature seems soothing; the Western landscape appears welcoming. And for the first time all day, we might experience solitude—even peacefulness.

The thousands of "tired, nerve-shaken, over-civilized people" who visited the World's Columbian Exposition were not unlike so many Americans of their day, according to naturalist John Muir. On the eve of the twentieth century, Americans faced a bewildering barrage of wrenching technological, social, and economic changes. For them, Jackson's Western photographs provided a geography of hope.

Muir, one of Jackson's contemporaries, was also fascinated by "fine, wild views" discovered on rambles in the natural world. Americans, he wrote in 1897, "are beginning to find that going to the mountains is going home; that wildness is a necessity; and that mountain parks and reservations are useful not only as fountains of timber and irrigating rivers, but as fountains of life."

THE VIEW FROM THE TWENTY-FIRST CENTURY

The actual Western experience was much more complicated and varied than the stories that Buffalo Bill or Turner told their audiences in the nineteenth century. Today, many historians prefer to think of the frontier not as a place where "civilization met savagery," but as a cultural crossroads where many different kinds of people—Indians, African Americans, Asians, Europeans, South and Central Americans, and women as well as men—lived temporarily or permanently.

The story of the frontier can be told from many different perspectives: from the standpoint of native inhabitants as well as Euro-American invaders, immigrants as well as emigrants, women as well as men, even land and animals as well as people. The story of the West is really about cultural contact, territorial conquest, settlement patterns, and social relations between many different kinds of people.

About 160 years ago, in 1846, Francis Parkman (1823–1893) from Boston decided to make the trip across country on the Oregon Trail. The sickly, twenty-three-year-old Harvard scholar wasn't exactly prepared for the rigor of the journey. He broke his already poor health but succeeded in fulfilling his dream to see the wilderness. Even though the place was scarcely populated, he decided while riding near Pikes

Peak in Colorado that one day cattle would replace buffalo and that farms would transform the landscape.

Almost thirty years later, in 1873, Parkman returned and was shocked by the changes he saw. Not only farms and cities but the "disenchanting screech of the locomotive" had invaded the Rockies. "The mountain trapper is no more," he wrote in the preface to *The Oregon Trail*. "And the grim romance of his hard, wild life is a memory of the past."

Many aspects of the West have changed since Parkman noticed the disappearance of the mountain trapper. But it's fair to say that the frontier is not really gone. The different people who inhabit the West are still trying to figure out how to live together. Many of the same issues involving farmers and ranchers, land sales and development, gold rushes and oil booms, government bureaucrats and taxpayers, speculators and settlers are still being played out. The frontier is far from over.

On August 25, 1940,
almost seventy years after his
first visit, Jackson toured
Yellowstone with his compact
35-mm Kodak Bantam.

"TO MAKE ALL KNOWN TO OTHERS"

*In living, as in art, rules are drawn from practice;
not the other way round."*
—William Henry Jackson
Time Exposure, 1940

Villiam Henry Jackson spent the remaining forty years of his life crisscrossing the continent and circling the globe taking photos. He eventually gave up his Denver business and went to Detroit to run the Detroit Publishing Company, creating color picture postcards and landscape reproductions. When the business went bankrupt in 1924, eighty-one-year-old Jackson returned to his very first career: painting. He soon discovered that he was considered "a genuine bit of history." At age ninety-three he was delighted to find himself assigned the job of creating Western historical murals for the Works Progress Administration in Washington, D.C.

Eventually he wrote his memoirs, moved to New York City, and became research secretary for the Oregon Trail Memorial Association, a job which happily took him back and forth across the country every summer. Throughout the latter part of his life, he continued to experiment with photography. In 1939, he tried color film for the first time. "All I need say is this," he later wrote, "if I were at the beginning of my career, I should wish to do everything in color." Now whenever he traveled, he used the latest camera: a small, compact 35-mm Kodak Bantam.

Jackson saw numerous changes, some happy, some tragic. His three children grew up, married, and had children and grandchildren of their own. Jackson's wife of forty-four years died in 1917. He watched the country convulsed by World War I and the misery of the Great Depression.

For many Americans, Jackson had become a connection to the West's legendary past. In newspapers and magazine feature stories he was called "the old time photographer and elderly explorer"—titles he seemed to relish. The man who bullwhacked on the Oregon Trail also traveled by airplane. The man who survived the Battle of Gettysburg also marched in a parade in Washington, D.C., on the eve of World War II. Jackson was proud to say that of the six Gettysburg survivors, he was the only one who walked in the parade on his own two legs.

When asked the reason for his remarkable longevity, he wrote, "I never took out enough time to get run down. There has always been so much to do tomorrow that I haven't ever relaxed to any great extent. I have been too busy doing interesting things and getting ready to do even more interesting things."

In 1941, at age ninety-eight, Jackson fell into an open areaway while strolling in New York City. This was an injury from which he never fully recovered. Merrill J. Mattes, who worked at the Scotts Bluff National Monument in Nebraska, recalled his trip to the hospital to visit white-bearded Jackson with his full head of silver hair. "Even there he still looked both ancient and distinguished," Mattes wrote, "briskly ordering nurses around."

Before his accident, Jackson had agreed to an unusual interview. He was ninety-eight years old when he sat before a newfangled "sound-reel recording" device and spoke into a microphone. The employee from the Department of the Interior asked Jackson what was the most interesting thing that happened to him in his entire experience in the West.

Jackson did not hesitate. "I always thought that the most interesting period in my life," he replied in a high, clear voice, "was the years I spent in the Hayden survey—to make all known to others."

Jackson died on June 30, 1942, just ten months short of his hundredth birthday. His legacy "to make all known to others" lives on in his photographs—each truly a window on the West.

GLOSSARY

albumen print—Photographic print made on paper coated with egg white and salt solution, which is sensitized with silver nitrate solution. Prints are made by exposing the paper to sunlight through a negative.

collodion process—A complex process for making negatives that involves a glass plate coated with a light-sensitive emulsion of guncotton dissolved in alcohol and ether and mixed with potassium iodide and potassium bromide. Also known as the wet-plate collodion process.

daguerreotype—The first practical photographic process, which was introduced in 1839 in Paris by Louis-Jacques-Mandé Daguerre. The process requires a silver-coated copper plate that has been sensitized with vapors of iodine. The plate is developed in mercury fumes after exposure in a camera. The resulting small, reflective, one-of-a-kind images have to be held up to the light at a certain angle to be seen. Images are sealed in glass to prevent deteriorating effects of atmosphere and handling.

dry tissue developing *or* **dry plate**—The successor to the wet-plate or collodion process, dry plates are glass sheets pre-coated with silver halides suspended in gelatin.

stereoview *or* **stereograph**—Photographs taken by a special camera with two lenses, which is used to take a pair of views at slightly different angles. The images are mounted side by side on a *stereo card* and viewed separately by each eye in a *stereoviewer* or *stereoscope*, which creates the illusion of three dimensions.

TIME LINE

1839 **First daguerreotype is invented in France; process attempted in America**

1843 William Henry Jackson is born in Keeseville, New York

1850 **Stereoscopic views produced by camera introduced commercially in the United States**

1851 **Collodion wet-plate glass negatives are introduced**

1858 Jackson begins job as photographic retouching artist

1862 Jackson volunteers as Union soldier in Civil War

1863 When his enlistment time ends, Jackson returns to civilian life as photographic retoucher

1865 Civil War ends

1866 After a fight with his fiancée, Jackson leaves for West

1867 Jackson drives oxen teams on Oregon Trail and herds wild horses from Los Angeles to Omaha. Discovers his former fiancée married a friend; decides to stay in Omaha. Opens Jackson Brothers' Studio and begins career as photographer

1868 Jackson makes series of Indian portraits in Omaha area

1869 Jackson marries Mollie Greer, then leaves for summer to photograph along line of Union Pacific—his first extensive landscape work; in Cheyenne he meets Ferdinand Vandeveer Hayden

1870 Jackson takes unpaid job with U.S. Geological and

Geographic Survey and travels as photographer to far southwest end of Wyoming Territory

1871   Jackson becomes official Hayden survey photographer; explores Yellowstone region

1872   After exploring Grand Tetons, Jackson returns to Yellowstone; Mollie Greer Jackson dies in childbirth

1873   Survey focuses on Rockies; Jackson takes picture of Mount of the Holy Cross; Jackson marries Emilie Painter

1874   Jackson works in southwestern Colorado, photographing Ute Indians, and discovers cliff ruins in Mancos Canyon near Mesa Verde

1875   Survey expands work in Mesa Verde region; Jackson makes his first mammoth plate negatives (20 x 25 inches)

1876   Hayden assigns Jackson job of creating model of Mancos Canyon ruins for Centennial Exposition in Philadelphia

1877   Jackson experiences setback when photos taken in southern Colorado, Arizona, and New Mexico are ruined during experiment with dry-process negatives

1878   Survey returns to Grand Tetons, Wind River Mountains, and Yellowstone; this is Hayden's last survey

1879   **Gelatin dry plates become commercially available**
Jackson opens Denver commercial photo studio specializing in landscapes and Western views

1889   **George Eastman begins production of nitrocellulose film**

1892   Jackson journeys along Santa Fe route with Thomas Moran, old Survey friend; also makes photo trip on B & O Railroad

1893   Economic depression hits. Jackson hired to photograph World's Columbian Exposition in Chicago

1894–6   Jackson travels with World's Transportation Commission through the Near and Far East, Australia, China, Siberia, and Russia

1897   Jackson joins Detroit Photographic Company, mass-market postcard and "view" company, taking his vast negative collection with him

1917   Wife, Emilie Painter Jackson, dies

1924   Detroit Publishing Company goes bankrupt; Jackson moves to Washington, D.C., and begins to paint again

1929   Jackson publishes *The Pioneer Photographer: Rocky Mountain Adventures with a Camera*; is appointed research secretary for Oregon Trail Memorial Association

1936   Jackson is hired by President Roosevelt's Works Progress Administration to create Survey murals

1937   Jackson is transferred to National Park Service to produce paintings for other national parks

1940   *Time Exposure*, Jackson's autobiography, is published

1942   Jackson, 99, dies in New York City

BIBLIOGRAPHY

Investigating the fascinating life and work of William Henry Jackson required delving into his extensive collection of diaries. While in Denver I found it especially thrilling to examine firsthand an early pocket-sized notebook hastily scrawled in pencil and illustrated with sketches of scenery and humorous profiles of fellow travelers. The worn cover showed signs of hard use. Where had the journal been? How many miles had it traveled? Somehow contact with this very personal keepsake made Jackson and his wide-ranging travels come to life for me.

I soon discovered that Jackson's diary collection is far from complete. Only portions are available for most eras of his long life. Some may have been destroyed. Others were probably misplaced. Unfortunately, a few diaries were altered, presumably by Jackson in his old age.

Pre-Survey and Civil War diaries are preserved by the New York Public Library Rare Books and Manuscript Collection. The Colorado Historical Society in Denver stores the diaries written during and after his Survey work. Also in Denver is a revealing collection of Jackson's correspondence.

LeRoy R. and Ann W. Hafen have edited a helpful book, *The Diaries of William Henry Jackson, Frontier Photographer, to California and Return, 1866–1867, and with the Hayden Surveys to the Central Rockies, 1873, and to the Utes and Cliff Dwellings, 1874.* Another source of many insights is *Time Exposure: The Autobiography of William Henry Jackson.* Although Jackson admitted in letters dating from 1940 that he had assistance on this autobiographical project from a "Mr. Brown" and from another editor, *Time Exposure* remains an illuminating portrait of an eventful life.

Jackson's enormous collection of photographs is scattered throughout the United States in archives, libraries, and art museums. Jackson occasionally purchased other photographers' work and did now always keep careful records. However, every effort has been made to verify photos used as Jackson's work. The United States Department of Interior Geological Survey (USGS) in Denver has a splendid collection of Indian photographs, early railroad images from 1869, and photographs from the Hayden expeditions. The Colorado State Historical Society stores Western views that were once part of the negative archives of Jackson's later enterprise, the Detroit Publishing Company. The Prints and Photographs Division of the Library of Congress serves as the principal repository for Jackson's post-Survey work. The Amon Carter Museum in Fort Worth, Texas, and the Museum of Natural History in Philadelphia have impressive, well-researched arrays of Jackson's images.

The Western History Room of the Denver Public Library and the Prints and Photographs Department of the Chicago Historical Society have many rare prints, illustrated albums, and publications from his later years. Equally fascinating are prints, early paintings, and sketches and photos held by the Scotts Bluff National Monument in Gering, Nebraska. I also made use of numerous annual reports published by the U.S. government, as part of Hayden's U.S. Geological and Geographical Surveys of the Territories. In 1874, 1875, and 1877 Jackson helped archaeologist William Henry Holmes sketch findings. He also wrote chapters or bulletins from 1874 through 1878, which appeared as part of the published findings.

A useful publication compiled by Thomas H. Harrell is *William H. Jackson: An Annotated Bibliography (1862–1995)* (Nevada City, CA: Carl Mautz Publishing, 1995), which provides chronological listings of numerous books and magazine articles by and about Jackson. Also essential is the meticulously researched book about Jackson's life and art by Peter B. Hales, *William Henry Jackson and the Transformation of the American Landscape.*

Because of the breadth of subjects covered in *Window on the West*, I made use of many different published resources. Especially helpful in exploring the West in broad overview are William H. and William N. Goetzmann's *The West of the Imagination*; Wallace Stegner's *Beyond the Hundredth Meridian*; Geoffry C. Ward's *The West: An Illustrated History* and Rodman Paul's *The Far West and the Great Plains in Transition: 1859–1900.*

Other noteworthy examinations of the West in light of recent scholarship are provided in editor Clyde A. Milner's *A New Significance: Re-Envisioning the History of the American West*; Richard Slotkin's *The Fatal Environment: Myth of Frontier in Age of Industry: 1800–1890*; Wallace Stegner's *The American West as Living Space*; and Richard White and Patricia Nelson Limerick's *The Frontier in American Culture.*

For information regarding the Gilded Age, valuable books include Ray Ginger's *Age of Excess: U.S. from 1877 to 1914*; Sean Dennis Cashman's *America in the Gilded Age, from the Death of Lincoln to the Rise of Theodore Roosevelt*; Alan Trachtenberg's *The Incorporation of American Culture and Society in the Gilded Age*; and Thomas J. Schlereth's *Victorian America: Transformations in Everyday Life, 1876–1915.*

Investigating the impact of photographs on the development of the West is well researched in editor William H. Truettner's *The West as America: Reinterpreting Images of the Frontier, 1820–1920.* A classic discussion of the development of photography in America is Robert Taft's *Photography and the American Scene: A Social History 1839–1889.* Also useful is Alan Trachtenberg's

Reading American Photographs: Images as History from Mathew Brady to Walker Evans and Alan Thomas's Time in a Frame. Two books on stereographs that are particularly insightful are William Culp Darrah's Stereo Views: A History of Stereographs in America and their Collection and editor Edward W. Earle's Points of View: The Stereograph in America.

There are many wonderful books about the development and impact of the railroad. Of special interest is Dee Brown's Hear That Lonesome Whistle Blow: Railroads in the West; Sandra Phillips's Crossing the Frontier: Photographs of the Developing West, 1849 to the Present; and Susan Danly Walther's The Railroad in the American Landscape, 1850–1950.

Books about specific Native American issues abound. Fascinating overviews are provided by Robert M. Utley's The Indian Frontier of the American West: 1846–1890; editor Peter Nabokov's Native American Testimony; and David A. Dary's The Buffalo Book: The Full Saga of the American Animal.

Exploration of the West and the importance of the Surveys are well covered in W. J. Naef and J. N. Wood's Era of Exploration: The Rise of Landscape Photography in the American West, 1860–1885; William H. Goetzmann's Exploration and Empire: The Explorer and the Scientist in the Winning of the American West; and chief photographer Mark Klett's Second View: The Rephotographic Survey Project.

Interesting interpretations of the effect of the railroad in the West and the railroad's impact on art and the popular imagination are found in Leo Marx's Machine in the Garden: Technology and the Pastoral Ideal in America; Roderick Nash's Wilderness and the American Mind; Barbara Novak's Nature and Culture and the American Landscape and Painting, 1825–1875; Jules David Prown's Discovered Lands, Invented Pasts: Transforming Visions of the American West; and Henry Nash Smith's Virgin Land: The American West as Symbol and Myth.

Tourism, its development and impact are well discussed in Earl Pomeroy's In Search of the Golden West: The Tourist in Western America, as well as in Wolfgang Schivelbusch's The Railway Journey: Trains and Travel in the Nineteenth Century. Finally, of special note is Terry W. Mangan's Colorado on Glass: Colorado's First Half Century as Seen by the Camera, which provides a wonderful view of Jackson's Colorado work.

The following alphabetical bibliography is divided into books and articles.

Books

Ambrose, Stephen E. Crazy Horse and Custer: The Parallel Lives of Two American Warriors. Garden City, New York: Doubleday & Co., 1975.

Anderson, Nancy K. Thomas Moran. New Haven, Conn.: Yale University Press, 1997.

Applebaum, Stanley. The Chicago World's Fair of 1893. New York: Dover Publications, 1980.

Armitage, Susan, ed. The Women's West. Norman, Okla.: University of Oklahoma Press, 1987.

Badger, R. Reid. The Great American Fair: The World's Columbian Exposition and American Culture. Chicago: N. Hall, 1979.

Bancroft, Caroline. Estes Park and Grand Lake. Boulder, Colo.: Grand Lake Historical Society, 1968.

Bassford, Amy O. Home Thoughts From Afar: Letters of Thomas Moran to Mary Nimmo Moran. East Hampton, N.Y.: East Hampton Free Library, 1967.

Billington, Ray Allen. The Far Western Frontier, 1830–1860. New York: Harper & Brothers, 1956.

Bird, Isabella. A Lady's Life in the Rocky Mountains. Norman, Okla.: University of Oklahoma Press, 1960.

Black, Robert C. Island in the Rockies. Granby, Colo.: Grand County Pioneer Society, 1969.

Bowen, Exra, ed. This Fabulous Century: 1870–1890. New York: Time-Life Books, 1970.

Brown, Dee. The American West. New York: Touchstone, Simon & Schuster, 1994.

——. Hear That Lonesome Whistle Blow: Railroads in the West. New York: Touchstone, Simon & Schuster, 1977.

Brown, Julie K. Contesting Images: Photography and the World's Columbian Exposition. Tucson: The University of Arizona Press, 1994.

Brown, Mark H., and W. R. Felton. The Frontier Years, L. A. Huffman, Photographer of the Plains. New York: Henry Holt and Company, 1955.

Burg, David F. Chicago's White City. Lexington, Ky.: University of Kentucky Press, 1976.

Cashman, Sean Dennis. *America in the Gilded Age, from the Death of Lincoln to the Rise of Theodore Roosevelt.* New York: New York University Press, 1993.

Catton, Bruce. *The Civil War.* New York: American Heritage Publishing Co., 1982.

Chapman, J. G. *The American Drawing Book: A Manual for the Amateur and Basis of Study for the Professional Artist.* New York: Barnes, 1854.

Chevalier, Michel. *Society, Manners and Politics in the United States.* Boston: Weeks, Jordan & Co., 1839.

Chiaramonte, Giovanni. *The Story of Photography: An Illustrated History.* Milan: Aperture, 1983.

Connell, Evan S. *Son of the Morning Star.* San Francisco: North Point Press, 1984.

Dallas, Sandra. *Colorado Ghost Towns and Mining Camps.* Norman, Okla.: University of Oklahoma Press, 1985.

Darrah, William Culp. *Stereo Views: A History of Stereographs in America and their Collection.* Gettysburg, Pa.: privately published, 1964.

Dary, David A. *The Buffalo Book: The Full Saga of the American Animal.* Athens, Ohio: Swallow Press Ohio University Press, 1989.

Dickinson, Anna E. *A Ragged Register.* New York: Harper & Brothers, 1879.

Duniway, David C., ed. *Covered Wagon Women: Diaries and Letters from Western Trails, 1852,* vol. 5. Lincoln, Nebr.: University of Nebraska Press, 1986.

Earle, Edward W., ed. *Points of View: The Stereograph in America: A Cultural History.* Rochester, N.Y.: Visual Studies Workshop Press, 1979.

Freedman, Russell. *Children of the Wild West.* New York: Houghton Mifflin, 1983.

Ginger, Ray. *Age of Excess: U.S. from 1877 to 1914.* New York: Macmillan, 1975.

Goetzmann, William H. *Exploration and Empire: The Explorer and the Scientist in the Winning of the American West.* New York: W. W. Norton & Company, 1966.

Goetzmann, William H., and William N. Goetzmann. *The West of the Imagination.* New York: W. W. Norton & Co., 1986.

Golay, Michael. *To Gettysburg and Beyond: The Parallel Lives of Joshua Lawrence Chamberlain and Edward Porter Alexander.* New York: Crown Publishers, 1994.

Gripenberg, Alexandra. *A Half Year in the New World.* Newark, Del.: University of Delaware Press, 1954.

Hafen, LeRoy R., and Ann W. Hafen, eds. *The Diaries of William Henry Jackson, Frontier Photographer, to California and Return, 1866–1867, and with the Hayden Surveys to the Central Rockies, 1873, and to the Utes and Cliff Dwellings, 1874.* Glendale, Calif.: Arthur H. Clark Co., 1959.

Haines, A. L. *The Yellowstone Story: A History of Our First National Park,* 2 volumes. Niwot, Colo.: Colorado University Press, 1996.

Hales, Peter B. *William Henry Jackson and the Transformation of the American Landscape.* Philadelphia: Temple University Press, 1988.

Harrell, Thomas H. *William Henry Jackson: An Annotated Bibliography.* Nevada City: Carl Mautz Publishing, 1995.

Harris, Neil. *Grand Illusions, Chicago's World's Fair of 1893.* Chicago: Chicago Historical Society, 1993.

Hayden, F. V. *Sun Pictures of Rocky Mountain Scenery, with a Description of the Geographic and Geological Features, and Some Account of the Resources of the Great West.* New York: J. Bien, 1870.

Holbrook, Stewart H. *The Age of the Moguls.* New York: Doubleday & Co., 1953.

Hoxie, Frederick E. *Indians in American History.* Arlington Heights, Ill.: Horlan Davidson, Inc., 1988.

Hughes, Jim. *The Birth of a Century: Early Color Photographs of America.* New York: Tauris Parke Books, 1994.

Jackson, Clarence S. *Picture Maker of the Old West.* New York: Charles Scribner's Sons, 1947.

Jackson, Donald. *Letters of the Lewis and Clark Expedition, 1783–1854.* Urbana, Ill.: University of Illinois Press, 1962.

Jackson, William H. *Time Exposure: The Autobiography of William Henry Jackson.* New York: G. P. Putnam's Sons, 1940.

Jackson, William Henry. *Descriptive Catalog of Photographs of Native American Indians.* Miscellaneous Publications, no. 9. Washington, D.C.: Government Printing Office, 1877.

——. *Gems of Colorado Scenery.* Denver, Colo.: Frank S. Thayer, 1988.

——. *The Pioneer Photographer: Rocky Mountain Adventures with a Camera.* Madison, Wis.: Tamarak Press, 1979.

Jenkins, Reese V. *Images and Enterprise.* Baltimore: Johns Hopkins University Press, 1975.

Jones, William C., and Elizabeth B. Jones. *William Henry Jackson's Colorado*. Golden, Colo.: Colorado Railroad Museum, 1975.

Kipling, Rudyard. *From Sea to Sea: Letters of Travel*. New York: Doubleday, Page & Co., 1923.

Klett, Mark, chief photographer. *Second View: The Rephotographic Survey Project*. Albuquerque, N.M.: University of New Mexico Press, 1984.

Koldony, Annette. *The Land Before Her: Fantasy and Experience of American Frontiers, 1630–1860*. Chapel Hill, N.C.: University of North Carolina Press, 1984.

Larson, Robert W. *Red Cloud: Warrior-Statesman of the Lakota Sioux*. Norman, Okla.: University of Oklahoma Press, 1997.

Lavender, David. *David Lavender's Colorado*. Garden City, N.Y.: 1976.

———. *The Rockies*. New York: Harper & Row, 1968.

Leslie, Mrs. Frank. *California: A Pleasure Trip from Gotham to Golden Gate, April, May, June 1877*. Niewkoop, the Netherlands: B. DeGraaf, 1972.

Longfellow, Samuel, ed. *Life of Henry Wadsworth Longfellow with Extracts from His Journals and Correspondence*, vol. 2. Boston: Ticknor and Fields, 1886.

Lowie, Robert H. *Indians of the Plains*. Lincoln, Nebr.: University of Nebraska Press, 1982.

Luchetti, Cathy, and Carol Olwell. *Women of the West*. St. George, Utah: Antelope Island Press, 1982.

Mangan, Terry W. *Colorado on Glass: Colorado's First Half Century as Seen by the Camera*. Silverton, Colo.: Sundance, 1975.

Marx, Leo. *Machine in the Garden: Technology and the Pastoral Ideal in America*. New York: Oxford University Press, 1964.

Mautz, Carl. *Biographies of Western Photographers*. Nevada City, Calif.: Carl Mautz Publishers, 1997.

McFarland, Gerald. *A Scattered People: An American Family Moves West*. Amherst, Mass.: University of Massachusetts Press, 1985.

McPherson, James A. *Battle Cry of Freedom: Civil War Era*. New York: Oxford University Press, 1988.

Milner, Clyde A., ed. *A New Significance: Re-Envisioning the History of the American West*. New York: Oxford University Press, 1996.

Morgan, Ted. *A Shovel of Stars: The Making of the American West, 1800 to the Present*. New York: Simon & Schuster, 1995.

Muir, John. "The Wild Parks and Forest Reservations of the West, 1897," *John Muir: The Eight Wilderness Discovery Books*. Seattle: The Mountaineers, 1992.

Nabokov, Peter, ed. *Native American Testimony*. New York: Viking, 1991.

Naef, W. J., and J. N. Wood. *Era of Exploration: The Rise of Landscape Photography in the American West, 1860–1885*. New York: Metropolitan Museum of Art, 1975.

Nash, Roderick. *Wilderness and the American Mind*. New Haven, Conn.: Yale University Press, 1967.

Neider, Charles. *The Great West: A Treasury of Firsthand Accounts*. New York: De Capo Press, 1997.

Nevins, Allan, ed. *Diary of Philip Hone, 1828–1851*, vol. 1. New York: Dodd Mead and Co., 1927.

Nobles, Gregory H. *American Frontiers, Cultural Encounters and Continental Conquest*. New York: Hill and Wang, 1997.

Norris, Frank. *The Octopus*. New York: Doubleday, Page & Co., 1901.

Novak, Barbara. *Nature and Culture and the American Landscape and Painting, 1825–1875*. New York: Oxford University Press, 1980.

Parkman, Frances. *The Oregon Trail*. Boston: Little, Brown and Co. 1873.

Paul, Rodman W. *Mining Frontiers of the Far West, 1848–1890*. New York: Holt, Rinehart and Winston, 1963.

Paul, Rodman. *The Far West and the Great Plains in Transition: 1859–1900*. New York: Harper & Row, 1988.

Pettit, Jan. *Utes: The Mountain People*. Boulder, Colo.: Johnson Books, 1990.

Phillips, Sandra. *Crossing the Frontier: Photographs of the Developing West, 1849 to the Present*. San Francisco: Chronicle Books, 1996.

Pomeroy, Earl. *In Search of the Golden West: The Tourist in Western America*. Lincoln, Nebr.: University of Nebraska Press, 1990.

Prown, Jules David. *Discovered Lands, Invented Pasts: Transforming Visions of the American West*. New Haven, Conn.: Yale University Press, 1992.

Rae, W. F. *Westward by Rail*. New York: D. Appleton and Co., 1871.

Reinhardt, Richard. *Out West on the Overland Train Across the Continent Excursion with Leslie's Magazine in 1879 and the Overland Trip in 1967*. Palo Alto, Calif.: America West Publishing Co., 1967.

Rinehart, Frederick R., ed. *Chronicles of Colorado*. Niwot, Colo.: Roberts Rinehart, 1965.

Rosa, Joseph G., and Robin May. *Buffalo Bill and His Wild West.* Lawrence, Kans.: University of Kansas Press, 1989.

Sandweiss, Martha A., ed. *Photography in Nineteenth-Century America.* New York: Harry N. Abrams, Inc., 1991.

Savage, Charles Roscoe. *Diaries.* (n.d., ca. 1894), located in Harry B. Lee Library, Brigham Young University, Provo, Utah. Cited in Hales, Peter B.

Schivelbusch, Wolfgang. *The Railway Journey: Trains and Travel in the Nineteenth Century.* New York: Urizeon Books, 1977.

Schlereth, Thomas J. *Victorian America: Transformations in Everyday Life, 1876–1915.* New York: HarperCollins, 1991.

Schlissel, Lillian, Byrd Gibbens, and Elizabeth Hampsten. *Far from Home: Families of the Westward Journey.* New York: Schocken Books, 1989.

Shearer, F. E., ed. *The Pacific Tourist: An Illustrated Guide.* New York: Adams & Bishop Publisher, 1879.

Slotkin, Richard. *The Fatal Environment: Myth of Frontier in Age of Industry: 1800–1890.* New York: Atheneum, 1985.

Smith, Henry Nash. *Virgin Land: The American West as Symbol and Myth.* Cambridge, Mass.: Harvard University Press, 1950.

Stegner, Wallace. *The American West as Living Space.* Ann Arbor, Mich.: University of Michigan Press, 1987.

——. *Beyond the Hundredth Meridian.* Boston: Houghton Mifflin, 1954.

Stevenson, Robert Louis. *Across the Plains.* New York: Charles Scribner's Sons, 1911.

Stilgoe, John R. *Metropolitan Corridor: Railroads and the American Scene.* New Haven, Conn.: Yale University Press, 1983.

Sutherland, Daniel E. *The Expansion of Everyday Life: 1860–1876.* New York: Harper & Row, 1989.

Taft, Robert. *Photography and the American Scene: A Social History 1839–1889.* New York: The Macmillan Co., 1938.

The White City. Chicago: The White City Art Co., 1894.

Thomas, Alan. *Time in a Frame: Photography and the Nineteenth-Century Mind.* New York: Schocken Books, 1977.

Trachtenberg, Alan. *The Incorporation of American Culture and Society in the Gilded Age.* New York: Hill and Wang, 1982.

——. *Reading American Photographs: Images as History from Mathew Brady to Walker Evans.* New York: Hill and Wang, 1989.

Truettner, William H., ed. *The West as America: Reinterpreting Images of the Frontier, 1820–1920.* Washington, D.C.: Smithsonian Institution Press, 1991.

Twain, Mark. *Roughing It.* New York: Harper & Brothers, 1871.

Ubbelohde, Carl. *A Colorado History.* Boulder, Colo.: Pruett Publishing Co., 1976.

Utley, Robert M. *The Indian Frontier of the American West: 1846–1890.* Albuquerque, N.Mex.: University of New Mexico Press, 1984.

Van Doren, Mark, ed. *The Portable Walt Whitman.* New York: Penguin Books, 1973.

Vestal, Stanley. *Sitting Bull: Champion of the Sioux.* Norman, Okla.: University of Oklahoma Press, 1989.

Villard, Henry. *The Past and Present of the Pikes Peak Gold Regions.* Princeton, N.J.: Princeton University Press, 1932.

Walther, Susan Danly. *The Railroad in the American Landscape, 1850–1950.* Wellesley, Mass.: Wellesley College Museum, 1981.

Ward, Geoffry C. *The West: An Illustrated History.* Boston: Little, Brown and Co., 1996.

Welling, William. *Photography in America: The Formative Years, 1839–1900.* New York: Thomas Y. Crowell, 1978.

Wellman, Paul I. *Death on the Prairie: The Thirty Years' Struggle for the Western Plains.* Lincoln, Nebr.: University of Nebraska Press, 1987.

White, Richard. *"It's Your Misfortune and None of My Own": A History of the American West.* Norman, Okla.: University of Oklahoma Press, 1991.

White, Richard, and Patricia Nelson Limerick. *The Frontier in American Culture.* Berkeley: University of California Press, 1994.

Whitman, Walt. *Specimen Days.* Boston: David R. Godine, 1971.

Willard, Frances E. *Writing Out My Heart: Journal 1855–96.* Edited by Carolyn Gifford. Chicago: University of Illinois Press, 1995.

William Henry Jackson (audiotape recording) Washington, D.C.: Department of the Interior, 1940.

Writers' Program, Works Project Administration. *The WPA Guide to 1930s Colorado.* Lawrence, Kans.: University of Kansas Press, 1987.

Writers' Program, Works Project Administration. *The WPA Guide to Wyoming.* New York: Oxford University Press, 1941.

Articles

Bossen, Howard. "A Tall Tale Retold: The Influence of the Photographs of William Henry Jackson on the Passage of the Yellowstone Park Act of 1872." *Studies in Visual Communication*, vol. 8, no. 1 (Winter 1982): 97–109.

"A Few Hints on the California Journey." *Scribner Monthly* (May–October 1873): 25–31.

Holmes, Oliver Wendell. "The Stereoscope and the Stereograph." *Atlantic Monthly*, vol. 3 (June 1859): 738–748.

Jackson, William H. "Field Work." *The Philadelphia Photographer*, vol. 12 (1875): 91–93.

———. "Ancient Ruins in Southwestern Colorado." In Hayden, F. V. (8th) *Annual Report of the United States Geological and Geographical Survey of the Territories, Embracing Colorado and Parts of Adjacent Territories; being a Report of the Progress of the Exploration for the year 1874*. Washington, D.C.: Government Printing Office (1876): 376–381.

———. "A Relation of Some of the Experiences of a Tenderfoot in Driving a Band of 'Broncos' from Los Angeles to Omaha, in the Year 1867." Written 1922. Colorado Historical Society, Denver, typescript.

———. "First Official Visit to the Cliff Dwellings." *Colorado Magazine*, vol. 1, no. 4 (May 1924): 151–160.

———. "Photographing the Colorado Rockies Fifty Years Ago." *Colorado Magazine*, vol. 3, no. 1 (March 1926): 11–12.

———. "Bullwhacking Across the Plains." Written 1931. Colorado Historical Society, Denver, typescript.

———. "With Moran in the Yellowstone: A Story of Exploration, Photography and Art." *Appalachia*, no. 12 (December 1936): 149–158.

———. "A Visit to the Los Pinos Indian Agency in 1874." *Colorado Magazine*, vol. 15, no. 6 (November 1938): 201–209.

———. *Additional diaries:* (from 1862) pre-Survey diaries and Civil War journals from the New York Public Library Rare Books and Manuscripts Collection; (from 1870) Survey diaries from the Colorado State Historical Society, Denver.

King, Frank B. "In Nature's Laboratory, Driving and Fishing in Yellowstone Park." *Overland Monthly*, vol. 29, no. 39 (1897): 594–603.

Masteller, Richard N. "Western Views in Eastern Parlors: The Contribution of the Stereograph Photographer to the Conquest of the West." *Prospects*, vol. 6 (1981): 55–71.

Moorehead, Warren. "The Passing of Red Cloud." *Kansas Historical Collection*, vol. 10 (1907–8): 298.

Moran, Thomas. "A Journey to the Devil's Tower in Wyoming, (Artists' Adventures)." *Century Illustrated Monthly Magazine*, vol. 47, new series 25 (January 1894): 450.

Nicol, John. "Photography at the World's Fair." *Photo Beacon*, vol. 5 (August 1893): 257.

Pattison, William D. "Westward by Rail with Professor Sedgwick: A Lantern Journey of 1873." *Quarterly of Historical Society of Southern California*, vol. 42, no. 4 (December 1960): 335–349.

"The Photographic Display at the World's Fair." *Photographic Times*, vol. 23 (July 28, 1893): 401.

Putnam, John H. "A Trip to the End of the Union Pacific in 1868" (letters). *Kansas Historical Quarterly*, vol. 13, no. 3 (August 1944): 196–203.

Richards, Bradley W. "Charles R. Savage, The Other Promontory Photographer." *Utah Historical Quarterly*, vol. 60, no. 2 (Spring 1992): 137–157.

Ryder, J. F. "Photography at the World's Fair." *Wilson's Photographic Magazine* (September 1893): 422–423.

"Stereoscope Views of the West." *The Philadelphia Photographer*, vol. 10, no. 115 (July 1873): 64.

Toll, Roger W. "The Hayden Survey in Colorado in 1873–74, Letters from James T. Gardiner to his Mother." *The Colorado Magazine*, vol. 6, no. 3 (May 1929): 146–156.

Turner, Frederick Jackson. "The Significance of the Frontier in American History." *Annual Report of the American Historical Association for the Year 1893*, Washington, D.C.: Government Printing Office (1894): 199–227.

Places to View Jackson's Work

Amon Carter Museum, 3501 Camp Bowie Boulevard, Fort Worth, Texas

76107. Phone: 817–738–1933

    Variety of Western views, Indians.

Chicago Historical Society Library, 1601 North Clark, Clark Street at North Avenue, Chicago, Illinois 60614. Phone: 312–642–5035

    World's Columbian Exposition photographs.

Colorado State Historical Society, 1300 Broadway, Denver, Colorado 80203. Phone: 303–866–3682

    The William Henry Jackson Collection. Denver: Colorado State Historical Society. This computer database contains the collection of prints and glass plates of images west of Mississippi. Accessible at the Historical Society.

Scotts Bluff National Monument, P.O. Box 27, Gering, Nebraska 69341–0027. Phone: 308–436–4340

    Wide range of Jackson's sketches, later paintings, photographs.

United States Geological Survey (USGS) Library, MS 914 Box 25046 Federal Center, Denver, Colorado 80225–0046. Phone: 303–236–1010

    Survey photographs.

Western History Room, Denver Public Library, 10 West 14 Avenue Parkway, Denver, Colorado 80204. Phone: 303–640–6200

    Sample books and Denver photographs.

On-line Resources

Photographs from William Henry Jackson and the Detroit Publishing Company, 1880–1920. Washington, D.C.: The Library of Congress, American Memory Project. Access available through the Internet:

    <http://lcweb2.loc.gov/detroit/dethome.html>

    Approximately 25,000 images, many taken by Jackson, others collected by him as part of his Detroit Publishing Company. Includes 900 mammoth plate images taken by Jackson in the 1880s and 1890s.

Acknowledgments

front jacket, Bad-Lands on Blacks Fork River, Courtesy Academy of Natural Sciences; *back jacket,* William Henry Jackson, George Ebling and W. H. Jackson, Courtesy Colorado State Historical Society (CSHS) #F-22877; *page ii,* Harry Yount, Courtesy United States Geological Service (USGS) #526; *page iv,* Temple of Isis, Courtesy CSHS #2257; *page vii,* "Photographing in High Places" on Table Mountain ledge, Courtesy USGS #172; *page viii,* Rugged country, Courtesy USGS #1340; *page ix,* Mount of the Holy Cross, Courtesy Library of Congress Lot 12685, # 19 OSF; *page xii,* Platte Cañon, Colorado, Courtesy Academy of Natural Sciences; *page 2,* Seventeen-year-old Jackson, Courtesy Scotts Bluff National Monument #2005; *page 3,* School children, Courtesy CSHS #F24153; *page 5,* Argentine Pass, Courtesy USGS #1271; *page 7,* Cowboys, Courtesy USGS #F3528; *page 8,* Silverton, Colorado, Courtesy Library of Congress #LCD413834; *page 9,* Notebook from 1862, Courtesy of New York Public Library Rare Books and Manuscript Division; *page 10,* "Winter Quarters," Courtesy Scotts Bluff National Monument #233; *page 13,* Promontory Point, Courtesy USGS #712; *page 15,* Georgetown, Colorado, Courtesy USGS #1272; *page 16,* Jackson inspecting glass plate, Courtesy Smithsonian Institute, Office of Anthropology, Bureau of American Ethnology Collection, Hayden Survey #1; *page 20,* Tower Falls, Courtesy USGS #78; *page 22,* Daguerreotype of unidentified girl, Courtesy Library of Congress, Repro #LC USZ61985; *page 23,* Reprinted from J. Thompson, editor, *A History and Handbook of Photography,* (1877); *page 25 (top),* Stereoscope (photograph by Joseph M. Guillette); *page 25 (bottom),* stereoscope card from the collection of G. W. Goodman; *page 26,* Trestlework stretched over Echo Canon, Courtesy USGS #23; *page 28,* Jackson advertisement, Courtesy Nebraska Historical Society; *page 29,* Twenty-seven-year-old Jackson, Courtesy Scotts Bluff National Monument #2004; *page 30,* Glacier Point, Yosemite, California, Courtesy CSHS #F40383; *page 34,* Travelers at Phantom Curve, Courtesy CSHS #2927; *page 38,* Cañon of the Rio de Las Animas, Courtesy Amon Carter Museum #P1971.94.18; *page 39,* Bridge over waters of Rio de Las Animas, Courtesy CSHS #126; *page 43,* Royal Gorge, Courtesy CSHS #WHJ 3282; *page 44,* Chugwater River in Platte County, Courtesy USGS #250; *page 46,* Dr. Ferdinand Vandeveer Hayden, Courtesy USGS #119; *page 48,* Surveyors Ada D. Wilson and Franklin Rhoda, Courtesy USGS #1111; *page 49,* "Killed by Indians," Courtesy USGS #246; *page 51,* 1871 camp study, Courtesy USGS #500; *page 52,* Moran at Mammoth Hot

Springs on Gardiner River, Courtesy East Hampton Library #EHL 647; *page 54*, Pack train on trail, Courtesy USGS #114; *page 55*, Moran on horseback, Courtesy East Hampton Library; *page 56*, Grand Canyon of the Yellowstone, Courtesy USGS #90; *page 57*, Giant Geyser, Courtesy CSHS #14960; *page 58*, Yellowstone River, Courtesy USGS #68; *page 59*, Fountain Geyser on the Lower Firehole River, Courtesy USGS #562; *page 61*, Emilie Painter Jackson, Courtesy USGS #1116; *page 62*, Waterfall at foot of Round Top Mountain, Courtesy USGS #436; *page 63*, "Potato John," Courtesy USGS #1644; *page 64*, Fisherman's cabin, Courtesy USGS #1053; *page 65*, Twin peaks of Gray and Torrey, Courtesy USGS #1234; *page 66*, Tepee of Chief Gi-He-Ga, Courtesy of Amon Carter Museum #P1967.3270; *page 69*, Skulls and bones in Albany County, Courtesy USGS #348; *page 71*, Ute in headdress, Courtesy CSHS #F28719; *page 73*, Chief Pe-ah and other leaders, Courtesy CSHS #F-28719; *page 74*, Encampment at Los Pinos in La Plata County, Courtesy USGS #1173; *page 78*, Encampment of Washakie, Shoshone chief, Courtesy CSHS #F-31591; *page 79*, Chipeta, Courtesy CSHS, #F40201; *page 81*, 1874 photography division, Courtesy USGS #359; *page 82*, Cliff dwellings near Mancos Canon, Courtesy USGS #603; *page 83 (left)*, Cliff Palace, Mesa Verde, Courtesy CSHS #4251; *page 83 (right)*, Manitou Canyon, Courtesy CSHS #2257; *page 84*, Elkton Mine, Courtesy CSHS #13835; *page 88*, Private railroad car, Courtesy Scotts Bluff National Monument #SCBL 1036; *page 89*, Corinne, Utah, Courtesy USGS #716; *page 90*, Oro City/Leadville, Courtesy USGS #1395; *page 92*, Hydraulic mining near Virginia City, Montana, Courtesy USGS #61; *page 94*, Grand Canyon of the Colorado, Courtesy George Eastman House #GEH 18685; *page 96*, Bright Angel Trail, Courtesy CSHS #32799; *page 99*, Devil's Tower, Courtesy Library of Congress Lot 12690 no. 8H; *page 100 & 101*, Mammoth Hot Springs Hotel, Courtesy Library of Congress LC USZ62-93668LLC; *page 102*, 1878 photo of Mammoth Hot Springs Lower Basin, Courtesy USGS #518; *page 106*, Transportation Building, Courtesy Chicago Historical Society #CHi-17129; *page 108*, Court of Honor, Courtesy Chicago Historical Society #ICHi-17132; *page 109*, Buffalo Bill's Wild West, Courtesy Buffalo Bill Historical Center #1.69.108; *page 110*, Annie Oakley, Courtesy Buffalo Bill Historical Center #P.69.73; *page 114 (left)*, William Henry Jackson, 1895, Courtesy CSHS #F21.068; *pages 114 & 115*, Lake De Amelia, Courtesy Library of Congress LC US Z62-93667 DLC; *page 118*, William Henry Jackson, 1940, Yellowstone, Courtesy Scotts Bluff National Monument #SCBL 2690.

Index

Page numbers in italic type refer to illustrations.